INTERMEDIATE 2 & HIGHER
Business Management
course notes – **2nd edition**

× Ann Miller ×

Text © 2006 Ann Miller
Design and layout © 2006 Leckie & Leckie
Cover images © Getty Images, Ingram Publishing and Caleb Rutherford

3rd edition, printed 2007

ISBN-13 978-1-84372-463-6

ISBN 1-84372-463-4

Published by
Leckie & Leckie Ltd, 3rd floor, 4 Queen Street, Edinburgh, EH2 1JE
Tel: 0131 220 6831 Fax: 0131 225 9987
enquiries@leckieandleckie.co.uk   www.leckieandleckie.co.uk

Special thanks to
Rebecca Faulkner (copy-edit), Derek McInally (content review), Caleb Rutherford (cover design), The Partnership Publishing Solutions Ltd (text design and layout), Tara Watson (proofreading)

A CIP Catalogue record for this book is available from the British Library.

Leckie & Leckie Ltd is a division of Huveaux plc.

CONTENTS

6 Operations

7 Financial Management

8 Human Resource Management

9 Key Terms and Solutions

INTRODUCTION

Welcome to Leckie & Leckie's **Intermediate 2 and Higher Business Management** *Course Notes*. This book should provide you with an invaluable tool to help you throughout your course. It will assist you with clear and concise points and explanations to complement your class work and assist you with your homework. It will also be extremely useful when revising for your internal assessments, prelims and the final exam.

This book will provide you with coverage of all topics within the **Intermediate 2 and Higher Business Management** courses. There are eight topics you will cover:

- Business in Contemporary Society
- Business Information and ICT
- Decision-Making in Business
- Internal Organisation
- Marketing
- Operations
- Financial Management
- Human Resource Management

Internal Assessment

Throughout your course you will be asked to sit internal assessments. There are three separate assessments that cover the following topics:

Business Enterprise: *Business in Contemporary Society*
Business Information and ICT
Decision-Making in Business

Business Decision Areas: Marketing and Operations

Business Decision Areas: Finance and Human Resource Management

Note: The Internal Organisation topic is not assessed in an internal assessment.

External Assessment

The final Business Management exam has two sections:

	Section 1 *Case Study with Questions*	*Section 2* *Extended Response Questions*	TOTAL
Higher	50 marks	50 marks	**100 marks**
Intermediate 2	25 marks	50 marks	**75 marks**

General Hints

- Allocate appropriate time to each section of the exam.
- Read all questions carefully.
- Check the question several times whilst writing your answer to ensure you don't stray from the point.
- Check the marks allocated to each question. Include **at least** that number of points in your answer (i.e. if a question is worth 6 marks, write at least 6 points).
- If you answer in bullet points be careful your answers are not too brief. Leave a couple of lines blank between each point to allow you to go back and add to your points.
- Pay attention to the command word in the question to ensure that you answer appropriately. A list of SQA command words for Business Management and their meanings are shown below.

Intermediate 2

Command word	Definition
Compare	Identify similarities and differences between two or more factors
Define	Give a clear meaning
Describe	Provide a thorough description
Distinguish	Identify the differences between two or more factors
Explain	Give details about how and why something is as it is
Give	Pick some key factors and name them
Identify	Give the name or identifying characteristics of something
Name	Identify or make a list
Outline	State the main features
Suggest	State a possible reason or course of action (no development required)

Higher

Command word	Definition
Compare	Identify similarities and differences between two or more factors
Describe	Provide a thorough description
Discuss	Examine closely, taking account of strengths and weaknesses in an argument; offer reasons for and against
Distinguish	Identify the differences between two or more factors
Explain	Give a detailed response (definition and explanation) as to how/why something may benefit/hinder
Identify	Give the name or identifying characteristics of something
Justify	Give reasons to support suggestions and conclusions
Outline	State the main features

Hints for Section 1 *Case Study and Questions*	*Hints for Section 2* *Extended Response Questions*

Hints for Section 1
Case Study and Questions

- Read the questions first before reading the case study.

- Whilst reading the case study highlight any relevant information (bearing in mind the questions).

- Question 1 will relate to the case study and will be worth a maximum of 10 marks. Headings will be given for you to use in your answer. Use the headings given or you will be unable to gain all 10 marks.

- Answer all questions.

Hints for Section 2
Extended Response Questions

- Answer two questions only.

- Ensure that you can answer all parts of the questions you have chosen.

- Include any relevant diagrams in organisation structure, stock, product life-cycle or product mix questions. Label your diagrams.

- You must remember that in the final exam all Extended Response Questions in Section 2 are integrated. Each of the five questions you can choose from will include questions from a variety of topic areas.

How to Use this Book

Higher only

Course content is specific to Higher only.

Key Terms

These will enable you to build up a comprehensive bank of terms used within Business Management. They can be found on pages 113–115. You could use these as a revision technique where you revise a section of the notes then from memory write a definition of each term. It can then be expanded to include any other relevant information about that term for fuller revision, e.g. advantages and disadvantages.

Case Study

Fuller, more detailed examples given to illustrate points in the text.

Quick Questions

In a large topic there will be quick questions throughout the topic. In short topics you will find these questions at the end of a topic. These questions are not differentiated by Higher or Intermediate 2. Solutions can be found on pages 117–127.

Extended Response Questions

These are not past paper questions but should allow you to practice the type of responses you should make in the exam. The command words are shown in italics – always ensure your response matches the command word in the question. Solutions can be found on pages 129–150.

Study and Exam Hints

Business activity	involves using the four factors of production (see below) to produce goods and services which people require in order to obtain the things they want.

Cycle of Business

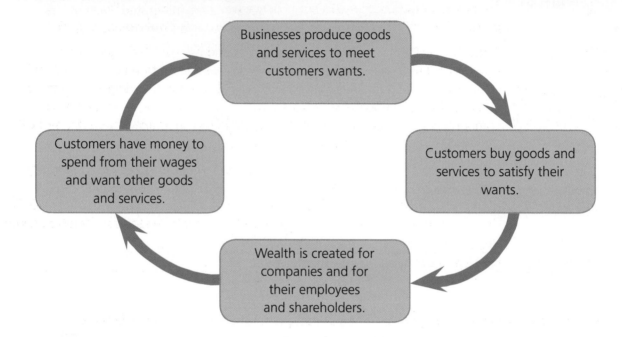

Factors of Production

Land

Land means the natural resources which businesses use (e.g. plot of land, coal, diamonds, forests, water, wood).

Labour

Labour means the workforce of a business.

Capital

Capital means the tools, machinery and equipment that a business owns or controls. It also includes the finance (money) that the owner has invested in the business.

Enterprise

Enterprise means the business ideas that an entrepreneur or owner has on how to use land, labour and capital in her/his business.

Sectors of Business Activity

Businesses can be grouped into sectors according to the types of product they produce or service they provide.

Primary sector

Businesses in this category grow products or extract resources from the ground (e.g. mining, farming, forestry).

Secondary sector

Businesses in this category manufacture products (e.g. shipbuilding, construction, factories).

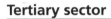

Tertiary sector

Businesses in this category do not produce a product but provide a service (e.g. shops, hotels, window cleaners, banks).

Since the 1960s the secondary sector in Scotland has declined significantly, resulting in fewer manufacturing firms. There has been a significant reduction in steel factories, shipbuilding and mills. This has been due to changes in customer demand, lack of competitiveness amongst Scottish manufacturers, increasing competition from abroad, lack of investment in manufacturing, the effects of UK Government policies and trade union practices.

The tertiary (service) sector has grown at the expense of the primary and secondary sectors in the UK. For example, whilst farming, mining, shipbuilding and steel production have declined significantly over the last 40 years in Scotland, businesses in the service sector (e.g. in tourism, finance and retailing) have seen considerable growth.

Private Sector Organisations

Private sector organisations are owned by private individuals with the prime objective of making a profit.

Type of organisation and its characteristics

Sole trader/ self employed

Definition

A sole trader is a one-owner business (it is owned and controlled by one person). Most small businesses are sole traders (e.g. hairdressers).

✔ Advantages ✔	✘ Disadvantages ✘
■ All profits kept by owner. ■ Owner has complete control over all decisions. ■ Owner can choose hours of work/holidays. ■ More personal service offered to customers. ■ Very easy to set up.	■ Owner has unlimited liability. ■ Available finance is restricted. ■ Owner has no one to share decisions/ problems with. ■ Owner has no one to share workload with. ■ Work may stop if owner is ill/on holiday.

Finance is available from: owner's savings, business's retained profits, bank loan, bank overdraft, government grants, trade credit and debt factoring.

Possible **objectives** might include: to survive; to maximise profits; to improve owner's personal status; to have a good image in the community.

Partnership

Definition

A partnership is a business with two to twenty partners – people who own and control the business together. The partners have to produce a Partnership Agreement which states each partner's rights and procedures to be followed when any partner joins, leaves or dies.

✔ Advantages ✔	✘ Disadvantages ✘
■ Partners can bring in different areas of expertise. ■ More finance available. ■ Workload can be shared. ■ Partners in a stronger position than a sole trader to raise finance from lenders.	■ Partners have unlimited liability. ■ Profits have to be shared between partners. ■ Partners may disagree. ■ If one partner dies or leaves, a new Partnership Agreement needs to be set up.

Finance is available from: partners' savings, partnership profits from previous years, inviting a new partner to join, bank loan, bank overdraft, government grants, trade credit and debt factoring.

Possible **objectives** might include the same objectives as those of a sole trader.

Private limited company

Definition

A private limited company (Ltd) is a company whose shares are owned privately (i.e. are not available to the public on the Stock Market). It has a minimum of one shareholder. It is owned by the shareholder(s) and run by a director or a board of directors. A shareholder can be a director. There must be a minimum of one director and one company secretary (who keeps all shareholder and company records). The company has to produce a Memorandum of Association and Articles of Association that state the company's details, responsibilities of directors and shareholders' rights. Private limited companies tend to be family businesses. Mackays Stores Ltd and Baxters Food Group Ltd are examples of private limited companies which are family owned.

✔ Advantages ✔	✘ Disadvantages ✘
■ Shareholders have limited liability. ■ Control of company not lost to outsiders. ■ More finance can be raised from shareholders and lenders. ■ Significant experience and expertise from shareholders and directors.	■ Profits shared amongst more people. ■ There is, as with a Partnership, a legal process in setting up the company. ■ Shares cannot be sold to the public. Therefore raising finance is more difficult than for a public limited company. ■ Firm has to abide by the requirements of the Companies Act. ■ Scottish-based firms must provide Companies House in Edinburgh with a copy of the annual accounts. They are then available to anyone who requests a copy.

Finance is available from: company profits from previous years, inviting a new shareholder to join, bank loan, bank overdraft, government grants, trade credit and debt factoring.

Possible **objectives** might include: to maximise profits; to grow; to have a strong status; to have the highest possible sales revenue.

CASE STUDY

Arnold Clark is one of the largest private limited companies in Scotland with over 135 UK car dealerships and over 7000 staff.

The business is owned entirely by Sir Arnold Clark and his family. A significant portion of the business is held in trust so that it cannot be sold, therefore avoiding loss of control to outsiders.

Sir Arnold Clark is the Chairman and Chief Executive with seven other directors (one of whom is also the Company Secretary). Not all directors are members of the Clark family.

Adapted from www.arnoldclark.com

Public limited company

Definition

A public limited company (plc) is a company whose shares are available for purchase by the public on the Stock Market. There must be a minimum of two shareholders and £50 000 share capital. A Memorandum of Association and Articles of Association that state the company's details, responsibilities of directors and shareholders' rights have to be produced. Shareholders own a plc.

A board of directors control the company. BT, Vodafone, Stagecoach and Celtic FC are all examples of plcs.

STAGECOACH *GROUP*

✔ Advantages ✔	✘ Disadvantages ✘
■ Huge amounts of finance can be raised. ■ Plcs often dominate their markets. ■ Easy to borrow money from lenders due to their large size.	■ Set-up costs of company may be high (e.g. they may have to produce top quality, detailed prospectuses and arrange underwriting). ■ Must abide by the Companies Act. ■ No control over who buys shares. ■ Must publish annual accounts.

Finance is available from: company profits from previous years, selling shares to the public, bank loan, bank overdraft, issue debentures, government grants, trade credit and debt factoring.

Possible **objectives** might include: to maximise profits; to expand output; to grow; to have a higher sales revenue than in previous years; to dominate their market; to have a strong image.

H **Higher**

Some plcs are very large, global companies. Where a plc has manufacturing plants in more than one country it is classed as a multinational. ICI, Honda and Shell are all multinationals. By being a multinational a company may:

● take advantage of economies of scale

● avoid restrictions on the number of products imported into a country

● avoid restricting legislation in its home country

● receive tax advantages and grants from other governments.

Type of organisation and its characteristics

Charities

The government regulates the activities of charities and keeps a Register of Charities. Charities are exempt from paying some taxes. Charities are often set up as trusts with no individual owner, where the overall control and management is dealt with by a Board of Trustees. Trustees are unpaid for their work in the charity. Volunteers often conduct much of the day-to-day fundraising. Examples of charities include Oxfam and Cancer Research UK.

Finance is available from: donations from the public and companies, government grants, Lottery grants, profits from their own shops, sale of goods through mail order and internet, raffles, fêtes and jumble sales, etc.

Possible **objectives** might include: to provide a service; to relieve poverty; to fund research into various medical conditions.

CASE STUDY

Children's Hospice Association Scotland
Sharing the Caring

The **Children's Hospice Association Scotland (CHAS)** is a registered Scottish charity which provides respite care for children with life limiting conditions.

CHAS runs the only children's hospices in Scotland, Rachel House in Kinross and Robin House in Balloch, as well as an at home service called Rachel House at Home for families in the North of Scotland.

These services are free of charge to families but in 2006/07 it will cost **CHAS** almost £5 million to run Rachel House, Robin House and Rachel House at Home service.

Adapted from www.chas.org.uk *and* www.oscr.org.uk

Voluntary organisations

Voluntary organisations are run and staffed by volunteers. Examples include the Scouts, youth clubs and some sports clubs. They bring together people with similar interests. They are run by a committee of elected volunteers.

These organisations can raise **finance** by applying for grants from the Lottery, Sports Council or local authorities. They may also charge a fee to become a member of their organisation or to use their facilities.

Quick Questions

1 What are the four factors of production?

2 Describe the three sectors of business activity.

3 Why have traditional secondary sector businesses declined in the last 50 years?

4 What is a sole trader and give three advantages and three disadvantages of this type of business for the owner?

5 What is a partnership and give three advantages and three disadvantages of this type of business?

6 Why might the partners in a partnership decide to change to a private limited company?

7 What advantages might a plc achieve by becoming a multinational organisation?

8 Describe the ownership and control of a charity.

9 Identify four possible sources of finance available to a charity.

10 Give four examples of voluntary organisations.

Publicly-funded organisations   are owned by the taxpayer and controlled by local or central government.

Type of organisation and its characteristics

Local government organisations

Local government/local councils provide a range of services including local education, recreation, housing and refuse collection. Local councils are set up by central government and are run on its behalf by locally elected councillors. The day-to-day running of services is organised by managers and employees of the council. A local council aims to meet local needs. It provides services that might be unprofitable if provided by private firms (e.g. library services).

Finance comes from central government, from business rates and from council tax. Councils also charge for some services such as leisure centre entrances and parking.

Possible **objectives** might include: to meet local needs; to provide a wide range of services; to make cost savings; to stick to agreed budgets.

Central government organisations

Westminster and the Scottish Parliament provide important national services. Services are provided by government departments such as the Treasury, Defence, Trade and Industry, Health and Transport.

Finance mainly comes from taxation. Policies and direction of departments come from elected politicians. Departments are run by employed civil servants.

Possible **objectives** might include: to provide a service; to improve society; to make effective use of funds; to make effective use of taxes.

Public corporations

These are companies that are owned by central government. A government minister appoints a chairperson and board of directors to run the company on the government's behalf. Public corporations include the BBC and Royal Mail Group.

✔ Advantages ✔

- Little competition.
- Service provided that may be unprofitable if provided by a private sector business.
- Provides a service to all consumers.

Hint

Do not confuse Publicly-Funded Organisations (e.g. NHS, Police and BBC) with Public Limited Companies (Marks & Spencer plc and Stagecoach plc).

Public corporations receive grants from the government and also raise **finance** from the public. The BBC charges the public for a TV licence and also sells videos/merchandise for programmes it produces.

Possible **objectives** might include: to provide a quality service; to make best use of funds; to be better than rivals; to serve the public interest.

Privatisation

Over the last 20 years, many public corporations have been privatised (sold) by the government to become public limited companies, with their shares traded on the Stock Market. Examples include British Airways, Scottish Power and British Telecom.

Governments sold these companies because:

- selling public corporations generated huge amounts of income for the government's Treasury
- some public corporations were poorly managed and not profitable. The government felt that, if sold off, they would become more competitive and profitable in the future
- the government wanted to increase share ownership and make the public have an interest in the success of the companies and the economy.

However:

- public corporations were often sold off too cheaply
- privatisation has not always led to greater competition.

Objectives

Objectives are goals (aims) which organisations have. Objectives are crucial to structured decision-making. Having objectives often motivates people in the organisation. Typical corporate objectives include:

- survival
- growth
- social and ethical responsibility
- provision of a service

- profit maximisation
- sales revenue maximisation
- specific managerial objectives.

Sales revenue maximisation
To achieve as much sales revenue as possible. This is popular with sales staff who receive bonuses or salaries according to sales made.

Higher

Profit maximisation
Where a private sector organisation aims to make as much profit as possible.

Growth
Many organisations aim to grow. A firm can aim to be more competitive, dominate the market and control prices. Growth can reduce the chance of failure.

Managerial objectives
Managers in an organisation often have their own specific aims (e.g. to increase their own salary, or to improve their position and responsibility).

Higher

Survival
Continuing to trade is vital, especially for a new business, and particularly where there is a recession, increased competition or reduced demand.

Social & ethical responsibilty
Many organisations aim to have a good image and be responsible towards customers, employees and suppliers. For example, Marks & Spencer has been working to improve its image with younger customers.

Provision of a service
A charity or local authority would have this objective.

Objectives depend on: the size of the organisation, the age of the organisation, the state of the economy and whether the organisation is in the public or the private sector.

Objectives may not be achieved due to: competition, environment, law, political situation, demands of shareholders, owners or society.

Many organisations also have among their stated aims to provide equal opportunities and to eliminate discrimination. Many organisations also aim to be environmentally friendly.

Stakeholders

Stakeholder	a person, organisation or group that has an interest in the success of an organisation.

Internal stakeholders	Their interest	Their influence
Shareholders	They want the firm to be profitable to provide them with good dividends and improved share value.	They can exert influence on the firm by voting for particular directors and approving dividend payments at the AGM.
Managers	They receive salaries and perhaps bonuses so they will want the organisation to be successful. They also want responsibility and status.	They make important decisions regarding hiring staff, product portfolio, etc. which may or may not be successful.
Employees	They want good salaries, job satisfaction, good working conditions and job security.	They can exert influence by the standard of their work and industrial relations (e.g. strikes).

External stakeholders	Their interest	Their influence
Customers	They want best quality products from organisations at the lowest prices.	Customers can choose to buy or not to buy an organisation's products or services. This influences the products and services an organisation makes/gives. Customers may recommend the organisation to friends/family.
Banks/other lenders	They will want to ensure that a business applying for a loan or with an existing loan has sufficient funds to make agreed repayments.	They can exert influence by granting or withholding loans, setting loan interest rates, or requesting repayment of loans if an organisation's ability to make repayments is in doubt.
Suppliers	A supplier will want a business to be a success to ensure repeat custom as they depend on their custom for survival.	They can exert influence by changing prices, credit periods and discounts offered.
Local community	Companies produce employment therefore generating wealth for an area, communities also have an interest that their environment is not harmed by noise or pollution.	They can exert influence by petitioning companies or making complaints to their local authority.

External stakeholders	Their interest	Their influence
Central government	They want businesses to be successful as they provide jobs, generate wealth and provide government with finance through taxes.	They can exert influence by producing legislation which businesses must comply with, e.g. health and safety, environmental laws, etc. Economic policies affect businesses, e.g. interest rates, inflation, etc. If interest rates are increased the cost of businesses borrowing finance increases.
Local government	They want businesses to be successful as they provide jobs and make payments of business rates. A council can receive a good image if it can attract and retain successful organisations. Local government also want the services it provides, e.g. schools, to be successful, to meet central government targets, provide them with a good image and be able to justify budget spending.	They can exert influence on businesses by granting or not granting licences for hotels and pubs, providing subsidised premises, or granting planning permission. They also influence the services they provide, e.g. schools, by allocating funding from council budgets and setting operational policies for services.
Charity donors **H** *Higher*	Corporate donors will want a charity that they donate to to be successful as it may provide them with good public relations.	They can exert their influence on a charity by giving or not giving donations. Donors of large amounts of money may specify the use to which their donation is put.
Taxpayers **H** *Higher*	They have an interest in publicly funded organisations to ensure that the taxes that they paid are used effectively.	They exert influence by voting for political parties at national and local government elections.

Conflict between stakeholders

As stakeholders do not all have the same interest in an organisation, conflict may arise between different stakeholders. For example, a business may want to maximise profits, whereas its customers will want to buy goods at the lowest prices. A business may want to build a new factory, but the local community may object as it could harm their local environment. The owners of a business may want to close a factory to cut costs but employees will not want to lose their jobs.

Entrepreneur	an individual who develops a business idea and combines the factors of production (i.e. land, labour, capital and enterprise) in order to produce a good or provide a service.

Entrepreneurs tend to be risk takers and use their initiative. They initially make all the business decisions from raising finance to hiring staff, so they have to be good decision-makers. Richard Branson (of Virgin Group), Duncan Bannatyne (of Bannatyne Fitness Centres) and Michelle Mone (of MJM International, makers of the Ultimo Bra) are all well-known entrepreneurs who each started with a small business and made it grow.

Most entrepreneurs start as a small business and are responsible for all aspects of it – from marketing and production to dealing with suppliers. As the business grows, the role of the entrepreneur may alter as he/she will then have managers/employees to delegate responsibility to.

Alternatively, an entrepreneur can reduce the risks involved with starting a new business by buying a franchise.

All entrepreneurs are enterprising where they demonstrate a desire to undertake new ventures. Encouraging enterprise is important as small to medium-sized businesses are important in developing innovative new technologies and products that can compete in the global market.

CASE STUDY

In 1996 Michelle Mone set up Glasgow-based **MJM International** after developing a new type of bra. Its unique selling point (USP) was the use of gel-filled silicone pouches to maximise cleavage and comfort.

Initially she made all the decisions regarding product design, pricing and distribution. As the business has grown she has a team of managers that deal with the day-to-day decisions while she concentrates on the strategic direction of the business.

The business is now worth in excess of £40 million.

Adapted from www.ultimo.co.uk *and* www.michellemone.com

Franchising

Definition

A franchise is a business agreement that allows one business (the franchisee) to use another business's name and sell the other business's products or services (e.g. The Body Shop, MacDonalds and The British School of Motoring). The franchisee pays the franchiser (the business whose name is used) a percentage of annual turnover or a set royalty each year to use its name and sell its products/services. The franchisee and franchiser can set up in any type of business, i.e. a sole trader, partnership, etc.

✔ Advantages to the franchiser ✔	✘ Disadvantages to the franchiser ✘
■ Allows the franchiser to increase its market share without investing heavily. ■ Provides a reliable revenue (the franchiser will receive a percentage of the turnover or a set royalty payment each year). ■ Risks and uncertainty are shared between the franchiser and the franchisee.	■ The franchiser only receives a share of the profits. ■ Profits dependent on the ability of franchisees. ■ Reputation of the whole franchise is dependent on individual franchisees.

✔ Advantages to the franchisee ✔	✘ Disadvantages to the franchisee ✘
■ The franchiser may advertise nationally, therefore little advertising needs to be done by the franchisee. ■ The risk of business failure is reduced as the business already has an established trading record and presence in the market. ■ The franchiser may carry out training and administration.	■ Products, selling prices and store layout may be dictated, stifling franchisee initiative. ■ A royalty payment or percentage of revenue has to be paid to franchiser. ■ The franchiser might not renew the franchise after a certain time. ■ Can be costly to purchase a successful franchise.

CASE STUDY

Domino's Pizza has more than 8000 franchise stores worldwide producing and delivering takeaway pizzas. A potential franchisee with **Domino's Pizza** will need to have approximately £230 000 startup capital. This includes construction and equipment costs and also entitles them to support regarding location, store design and construction, training, marketing and administration. **Domino's Pizza** offer franchisees initial training and the use of a consultant near the launch to assist with recruitment, training staff, marketing and pricing. Ongoing training throughout the agreement period which is normally 10 years is provided.

10.5% of annual sales are paid to the franchiser as a royalty and funding for national advertising campaigns.

Adapted from www.whichfranchise.com

Quick Questions

1 Give two reasons why the government sold many publicly funded organisations.
2 Identify three objectives a plc may have.
3 Choose a charity you know and give three objectives that charity may have.
4 Why might an organisation not achieve its objectives?
5 Name two internal stakeholders and explain each stakeholder's interest in an organisation.
6 Identify three stakeholders that would have an interest in a charity. Explain how each stakeholder can influence how a charity operates.
7 What is the role of an entrepreneur?
8 Why might the role of an entrepreneur change as their business grows?
9 What is a franchise?
10 Why might an individual setting up in business for the first time decide to buy a franchise?

What is a Manager?

It is the responsibility of managers to ensure the organisation achieves its objectives.

Functions of managers

Planning	Setting a plan of action for the future.
Organising	Collecting and arranging resources to meet plans.
Commanding	Ensuring duties are done properly by informing staff of what they have to do.
Co-ordinating	Having staff and resources organised to achieve the plan.
Controlling	Making sure everything works according to the plan.

Skills a manager requires

Interpersonal	The relationship a manager has with others (e.g. to lead, to encourage, to liaise, to motivate).
Informational	The collecting and passing on of information (e.g. gathering data, processing data and communicating).
Decisional	Making different kinds of decisions (e.g. solving problems, allocating resources).

Sources of Finance

Businesses can access many different sources of finance. The source of finance used depends on what finance is required for, and for how long it is required. Sources include: bank loan; overdraft; hire purchase; retained profits; share issues; debentures; venture capital; grants; trade credit; factoring; leasing; selling an asset.

Short-term sources of finance	✔ Advantages ✔	✘ Disadvantages ✘
Bank overdraft	A customer can arrange to take out more money from their bank than they have in it. This is simple to arrange. The amounts borrowed can vary up to an agreed limit and it is relatively cheap as interest is only charged on the actual amount borrowed for the number of days borrowed.	Can work out expensive if used for a long time. If the limit is exceeded, the facility may be withdrawn immediately and expensive charges incurred.
Trade credit	Firms buy goods from suppliers and pay for them at a later date. This helps a business get through periods when cash flow is poor.	Discount for prompt payment is lost. If payment is made outwith the credit period, suppliers may be reluctant to sell more goods on credit.
Factoring	A business can sell its customer invoices to a factoring company for less than their value. This improves cash flow as advance payment of bills is made by the factor. The factor chases up the unpaid invoices, saving the company time and money doing this.	Factors tend to be interested only in large values and quantities of invoices as they charge per invoice. The business does not receive the full amount of the original invoice from the factor.

Short-term sources of finance	✔ Advantages ✔	✘ Disadvantages ✘
Grant	A source of finance from central or local government, the EU, local enterpise companies (LECs) or the Prince's Trust. It is often an incentive for a new business to set up in a particular area of high unemployment.	They are one-off payments that once received are not usually repeated.
Retained profits	Profits kept back from previous years can be used to purchase assets.	Companies that self-finance using retained profits often find it difficult to grow at the speed they would like.

Medium-term sources of finance	✔ Advantages ✔	✘ Disadvantages ✘
Bank loan	The bank agrees to lend a specific amount of money for a specific purpose for a specific period of time and agrees repayment instalments. This makes budgeting/ planning easier as repayments are made in regular, fixed instalments.	Small businesses tend to pay higher interest rates.
Leasing	A business can rent vehicles or equipment from a leasing company. This can be used to avoid using up limited finance on an outright purchase. Leased equipment can be changed when obsolete.	The business does not own the equipment. Rental charges can build up over a long period of time – it may work out to have been less expensive to buy in the first place.
Hire purchase	A deposit is made for a vehicle or equipment with the rest of the purchase price being paid for in instalments. The cost is spread, making it easier to afford. The piece of equipment is owned by the company at the end of the instalment period.	The goods are owned by the finance company until the last instalment is paid. It is an expensive form of borrowing.

Long-term sources of finance	✔ Advantages ✔	✗ Disadvantages ✗
Owner's savings	This can reduce the amount to be borrowed if funds are needed. It allows the owners to keep control without bringing in others.	Once invested, owner's capital can be difficult to withdraw and the owner's capital is at risk if the business fails (if the owner has unlimited liability).
Share issue	This source of finance is available to companies. Shareholders have limited liability. Shareholders usually receive an annual dividend in return for their investment. Very large sums can be raised. This does not need to be repaid.	The cost of issuing shares can be expensive and it is difficult to estimate an appropriate selling price of shares.
Debentures	This is a source of finance used by plcs. A debenture is a group of loans from individuals and/or other companies. Debenture holders receive fixed interest over the period of the loan and then receive the amount of the loan back at the end (e.g. after 25 years). Large amounts of finance can be raised.	Debenture interest must be paid even if the business makes a loss. If the business fails, debenture holders have a right to sell its assets in order to have the loan repaid.
Venture capital	Venture capitalists will often provide finance when banks decide a loan is too risky. Venture capitalists accept more risky loans.	Venture capitalists are usually only interested in very large loans. The fee for their service is often high and they often want part-ownership in exchange for finance.

Hint

If you are asked in a question to give sources of finance for a specific type of business make sure that your answers are relevant, e.g. if asked for a source of finance for a sole trader to expand, debentures would be inappropriate to include in your answer.

Sources of Assistance

A new or existing business can turn to a variety of different organisations for support and assistance.

Higher

Scottish Enterprise and Local Enterprise Companies

These are government-funded organisations set up to help business start-ups and existing companies to grow. They offer advice, training courses, provide contacts, assist with gaining grants and funding and promote exporting.

Careers Scotland

This organisation is part of Scottish Enterprise and provides assistance with recruitment and training, information on local labour markets and employment law.

Business Gateway

This is a Scottish Enterprise-funded organisation. It provides information on finance and grants, taxation, health and safety, IT and E-business, sales and marketing.

Local Authorities

Each local authority in Scotland may provide different business support depending on local circumstances. Some offer help in locating premises, local planning matters, loans and grants and subsidised premises.

European Union

Provide a range of grants.

Scottish Chamber of Commerce

This is a business support organisation that businesses can become members of. They provide seminars on a range of business topics, networking opportunities and encourage exporting and international trade.

Princes Youth Trust

This organisation gives advice, training and grants to young people starting a business.

Trade Associations

These provide advice in their area of business. Examples include the Association of British Travel Agents (ABTA) and the Institute of Plumbing.

Banks

These give advice on sources of finance and drawing up a business plan. Many produce a pack of information useful to small businesses.

Inland Revenue

Give advice on taxation matters.

Lawyers and accountants

Give legal and financial advice.

Methods of Growth

A business can grow internally by opening up new sales outlets, hiring additional staff or developing new products. Alternatively, a business can grow by integrating with another to become larger and more powerful. If the integration is on equal terms, it is called a merger (e.g. Cadburys and Schweppes merged to form Cadbury Schweppes plc). If one firm takes control of another, it is called a takeover (e.g. Morrisons Supermarkets took over Safeway in 2003.) There are three types of integration:

1. Horizontal integration

Firms producing the same type of product or providing the same type of service combine together (e.g. two florists merging). Goods/ services become cheaper due to bulk buying and lower administration costs. These firms tend to dominate the market, compete against smaller firms and finally raise prices.

2. Vertical integration

Firms at different stages of production in the same industry combine together (e.g. an oil refinery integrating with a petrol station).

Forward vertical integration occurs when a business takes over a customer. This allows a firm to increase profits and control supply and distribution of their product.

Backward vertical integration occurs when a business takes over a supplier. This gives a guaranteed source of stock. As stock will be cheaper, increased profits are possible.

3. Conglomerate (diversification) integration

This occurs when businesses operating in different markets merge. This reduces the risk of business failure. A firm may seek new opportunities it it fears loss of market share or competition. It makes a larger and more financially secure business.

There are a number of reasons why a business will want to grow. These include:

- to avoid being a takeover target
- to reduce the risk of business failure
- to become the market leader and dominate the market
- to increase profits
- to remove a competitor
- to be able to take advantages of economies of scale.

CASE STUDY

- **Mackie's Ltd** (makers of ice-cream) have expanded their product range to include milk shakes, iced fruit smoothies and ice cubes – internal growth.
- **Bank of Scotland** and **Halifax** merged to create **HBOS** in 2001 – horizontal integration.
- **Scottish & Newcastle** breweries bought a pub operator in northern England for just over £10 million in 2004 – vertical forward integration.
- **AB Foods** (makers of Silver Spoon Sugar) purchased a 51% stake in Illovo (the largest sugar cane producer in Africa) in 2006 – vertical backwards integration.
- **Royal Bank of Scotland** bought **Marriot Hotels** in 2006 – conglomerate integration.

Higher

De-integration

This occurs when a business cuts back on or sells minor areas of their business in order to concentrate on core areas. This also provides funds from selling off less profitable areas.

De-merger

This occurs when a business splits into two separate organisations to raise cash for investment. It concentrates its efforts on its core activities and cuts costs to make it more efficient. For example, BT Cellnet demerged in 2001 into two separate companies – BT and mmO_2. The mobile phone company O_2 is a brand of mmO_2.

Divestment

This occurs when a business sells its business assets or a subsidiary company to raise finance. For example, when Morrisons purchased Safeway they identified a number of surplus stores to divest. They have sold a number of stores to other supermarkets including Somerfield, Tesco and Lidl.

Asset stripping

This occurs when a business buys another and then sells off the profitable sections bit by bit, and closes down the loss-making sections. A business may be worth more when sold off bit by bit than for the sum of what it was purchased for. Asset stripping can sometimes happen following a hostile takeover.

Contracting out/outsourcing

This involves one firm hiring another to supply parts or to do part of a job instead of the firm doing it themselves. A manufacturer may contract a delivery company to deliver goods rather than do it themselves. Commonly outsourced work includes printing, electrical work, accountancy, legal services and catering. Businesses outsource work because they do not possess the specialist equipment or expertise for the task, because they do not have enough staff, or if a rush order for an important customer is needed.

✔ Advantages ✔	✘ Disadvantages ✘
■ Less equipment and labour required, saving money. ■ High quality work from outsourced business as it should have greater expertise and specialist equipment. ■ Outsourced business may provide service cheaper than inhouse. ■ Need only use service when required. ■ Allows a business to concentrate on core activities.	■ Less control over outsourced work. ■ Communication between businesses needs to be very clear. ■ May have to share sensitive information (accountancy and legal outsourcing).

Management buy-out and buy-in

A Management buy-out happens when top managers buy the business they work for from the current owners. The managers then own the business. Managers may wish to buy out the business to enable them to keep their jobs and to make the firm more efficient. The current owners may wish to sell the business to raise finance for themselves. There was a management buy-out of Odeon Cinemas from the Rank Group in 2000.

A Management buy-in happens when a group of managers from outside the business takes over the business and runs it. Gala Bingo Group was created after it was bought from Bass in 1997 in a management buy-in.

Internal Business Environment

Within a business there are many factors that can influence performance.

Internal factor	Example of how it can affect a business
Finance available	A lack of finance may mean that a business has to consider cost cutting measures such as staff redundancies, downsizing, delaying equipment replacement or new product developments.
Ability of staff	Expert and capable staff will be more productive in their work.
Information available	If a business possesses good quality market research information a business will be more capable of responding to consumer needs.
ICT availability	The degree of ICT used within a business can influence the quality and quantity of products produced.
Ability of management	Good decisions made by management can have a positive influence on a business.
Changes in costs	Increases in wage rates or stock thefts would have a negative impact on a business' profitability.

External Business Environment

A company ignores the external business environment at its peril. The external environment means those events that are outwith a company's control. All companies must react to changes in the external environment. They are summarised as PESTEC factors or pressures.

P Political factors
E Economic factors
S Social factors
T Technological factors
E Environmental factors
C Competitive factors

Political factors

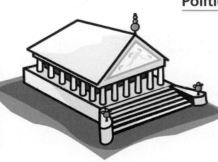

UK and EU laws and political decisions affect every business in the UK. For example, governments have set laws which ban advertising tobacco on television and disallow shops to sell alcohol on Sunday mornings. Businesses must comply with laws or face heavy legal penalties. Government policy can affect businesses by the government placing orders (e.g. orders for new defence ships to shipbuilding yards); setting taxation rates and providing infrastructure such as roads, rail, schools, hospitals.

In March 2006 new legislation was introduced in Scotland that made it illegal for people to smoke in confined public spaces.

In response to this many pubs and restaurants have introduced outdoor areas for smokers, more **No Smoking** signs have been put up and stubbing out bins provided.

Economic factors

Inflation, exchange rates and interest rates all affect businesses. If sterling (the UK currency) is high in comparison to other currencies, UK manufacturers struggle to sell products abroad. If the interest rate is high, the cost of borrowing for expansion is high. If there is a recession then unemployment rises and consumers have less income, which results in loss of sales for businesses. There is a rise in discounting and interest-free credit when there is a recession to encourage consumer spending.

Social factors

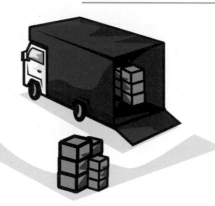

Demographic changes are movements in the size and distribution of the population. The following demographic changes have taken place over a period of time. Businesses take note of these to help them provide their customers with products that they want.

Demographic change	*Reaction of business*
The UK has a slow-growing population and an ageing one.	There has been a growth in products for the elderly. Some DIY stores now actively recruit older staff with practical DIY experience to assist customers.
The average age for a first-time mother is now 29.	Some businesses are now producing maternity products for more affluent first-time mothers.

Socio-cultural changes are changes in lifestyle and attitudes in society.

Socio-cultural change	*Reaction of business*
More women are now in work.	Supermarkets now sell more ready-made meals, stay open longer and provide internet shopping.
Increased concern about the environment.	Car manufacturers are developing cars that run on bio-fuel instead of petrol and diesel.
People have more leisure time.	Growth in hotels and restaurants as more people eat out and take more holidays.
Increased car ownership.	Increase in out-of-town shopping centres.
Increased awareness of the origins of products.	There has been a rise in fair trade and organic products.

Technological factors

Firms must keep up with new technology or face losing customers, sales, and profits. For example, they must use email, the internet and databases to attract customers. Some businesses also use new technology to reduce costs in production lines.

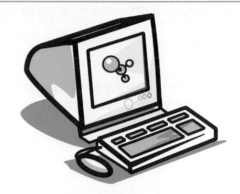

Environmental factors

Environmental factors could include storms, floods, pollution or noise. Some businesses have been severely affected by flooding in recent years. They have had to close and refurbish. This is an environmental event over which they have little control.

Competitive factors

Most businesses face domestic and foreign competition that has an influence on the way they operate. For example, Littlewoods Football Pools was affected when the National Lottery was introduced, so had to alter its selling and promotional techniques.

Changing Business Environment

Increasing significance of multinationals

Multinational companies are now expanding into markets in emerging countries. This creates global brands that dominate the market and deter new competition from entering. This continues to make multinational companies extremely powerful and dominant. See page 11 for additional details.

Publicly-funded organisations becoming more business orientated

Publicly-funded organisations such as the NHS are now more accountable to the government and the taxpayer than they once were. They have increasingly become in charge of their own finances and have to ensure that they meet agreed budgets. Business managers are employed to control the organisation. They have increasingly employed business practices such as appraisal, outsourcing and best practice benchmarking.

Importance of small firms

An SME (small to medium enterprise) is one which employs 250 staff or less. In 2004 SMEs accounted for 99% of all enterprises and provided 53% of all jobs in Scotland. SMEs play a vital role in the economy by providing employment, income, new ideas, products and services. SME numbers may continue to be driven up by:

- growth in e-commerce making it easy for small businesses to start up and find a market for their products

- outsourcing from large companies and the public sector

- promotion and encouragement of entrepreneurs

- a growing population of experienced over-50s wanting to start their own business.

Downsizing

There has been an increasing trend in recent years for companies to downsize. Downsizing is a measure of reducing the staff employed in an organisation to reduce costs and improve competitiveness. Many manufacturing companies have downsized their UK production only to move their manufacturing to cheaper, low cost countries in Asia. See page 50 for additional details.

Importance and growth of franchising

The franchising sector in the UK is very important to the economy. In 2005 it employed approximately 330 000 people with an annual turnover of £9.1 billion. The number of franchise outlets is growing in the UK with the number being unsuccessful declining. See pages 17–18 for additional details.

O————— **Quick Questions** —————O

1   What is a bank overdraft and a bank loan?
2   Share issues and debentures can generate large amounts of finance for a business. Describe each method of finance.
3   Outline three suitable sources of assistance an entrepreneur starting a new business could access.
4   Give five reasons why growth may be important for an organisation.
5   Describe three methods of growth.
6   Identify two advantages and two disadvantages of outsourcing.
7   Identify the internal factors that could influence an organisation.
8   Outline each of the PESTEC factors.
9   Distinguish between demographic and socio-cultural changes.
10 Identify the ways that the business environment has changed in recent years.

INTERMEDIATE 2

1 *Name* three types of private sector organisations. *Give* one
advantage and one disadvantage of each. (9 marks)

2 *Identify* three stakeholders that would have an interest in a public
limited company (plc) and three different stakeholders that would have
an interest in a publicly funded organisation such as an NHS Trust.
Describe how each stakeholder could influence the decisions of
each organisation. (12 marks)

3 *Describe* what is meant by the term 'entrepreneur'. (1 mark)

4 *Describe* the term 'franchise'. *Give* two advantages and
two disadvantages of franchising to
i) the franchisee and
ii) the franchiser. (9 marks)

5 *Describe* two sources of finance a sole trader could use to fund
the purchase of two new delivery vans. (4 marks)

6 *Identify* and *describe* three external factors that could influence
organisational success. (6 marks)

HIGHER

1 *Compare* the ownership and control of a partnership and a private limited
company. (3 marks)

2 *Describe* the objectives that a publicly-funded organisation such as the police
force (Fife Constabulary) may have. (3 marks)

3 *Describe* the interest that three external stakeholders would have in
a small six-bedroom hotel. *Describe* how each could influence the
operation of the hotel. (6 marks)

4 AG Barr (manufacturers of Irn Bru) is a plc. *Describe* three sources of
finance that a plc could use to finance the building of a new
factory. *Justify* your choices. (6 marks)

5 Many UK businesses are interested in entering into new emerging
markets in the Far East. *Describe* the different agencies that an
existing business could approach to assist with this. (4 marks)

6 News headline: BUTTERCREME DAIRY TO GROW
i) *Suggest* reasons why Buttercreme may want to grow. (3 marks)
ii) *Identify* and *describe* two methods of growth that would allow
Buttercreme to achieve its objectives. (4 marks)
iii) *Explain* how four of the following factors could affect Buttercreme
who manufacture a range of quality, high price,
full-fat butter:
Economic
Social
Technological
Environmental
Competitive
Internal (8 marks)

Hint

If asked to 'compare' in a question use the
word 'whereas' in each sentence where a
difference is being mentioned, e.g. a sole
trader has one owner whereas a partnership
can have between two and twenty owners.
Mention similarities, i.e. owners in a sole
trader and partnership both have unlimited
liability.

Data	is a collection of facts or quantities that has been assembled in some formal manner with the objective of processing it into specific information.

Information	is data that has been processed into a form that assists decision-making and planning.

Sources of Information

Sources of information	Strengths	Weaknesses
Primary information has been researched directly by an organisation for its own purposes, usually by observation, interview or questionnaire.	Information gained is first-hand and should be correct for the purpose for which it was gathered. Information can be kept private. Likely to be up-to-date. Source of the information is known.	Market research costs may be high. Research may be flawed (e.g. too small a sample; or leading questions used). Respondents may have lied. May be difficult and time consuming to collect. May have researcher bias.
Secondary information is gathered from published sources such as newspapers, textbooks, the internet and magazines.	Can be inexpensive and easy to access. A wide variety of sources of secondary information is available.	Information gathered for one purpose and then used for another may not be relevant. May have author bias. May be out of date. Is available to competitors.
Internal information is information that has been taken from the organisation's internal records (e.g. financial records, personnel data).	Accurate information can be gained once an organisation has been established for several years. Accurate records can help set and achieve targets by revealing past performance. Easy to access.	Costs of setting up and producing personnel and wages records may be high. New organisations may not have internal information to access. Accurate records need to be kept – regular updating required.
External information is gathered from sources outside the organisation (e.g. from market research, government reports, newspapers, competitors' annual accounts).	Can give an organisation useful information about PESTEC factors. Easy to get and cheap.	Time-consuming to gather. May be out of date. Information gained may be unreliable or biased. Is available to competitors.

Written

Information in the form of text (e.g. letters, memos, reports, emails, minutes).

Good for passing on information to confirm verbal messages; good for passing on information to be kept and used later; easy to collect.

Oral

Verbal and sound information (e.g. from telephone calls, presentations, meetings and conversations or discussions).

Good for discussions, providing advice and simple instructions. It provides an immediate response. However, it is less formal than written information and can be easily forgotten.

Pictorial

Information in the form of pictures and photos.

Used for passing on information that can be easily remembered, making documents more attractive and to emphasise a point. However, a relevant picture which effectively illustrates a point may be hard to find.

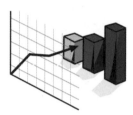

Graphical

Information in the form of graphs and charts (e.g. pie chart, line graph and bar graph).

Good way to display numerical information clearly, emphasise points and make comparisons (e.g. between monthly sales, company performance).

Numerical

Information in the form of numbers (often as tables and spreadsheets).

Allows an organisation to make financial predictions, perform calculations and analyse its financial performance, especially if using a spreadsheet.

Higher

Quantitative

Information that can be measured and which is normally expressed in numerical form.

Helps an organisation to analyse information and make accurate forecasts.

Qualitative

Information that is expressed in words and is descriptive, and involves judgements or opinions.

Allows an organisation to find out people's opinions about, for example, its products, advertising and new initiatives. However, this information can be biased and may be difficult to analyse.

Hint

Be clear about what is a **source** of information and what is a **type** of information. It is easy to confuse these in an exam.

Value of Information

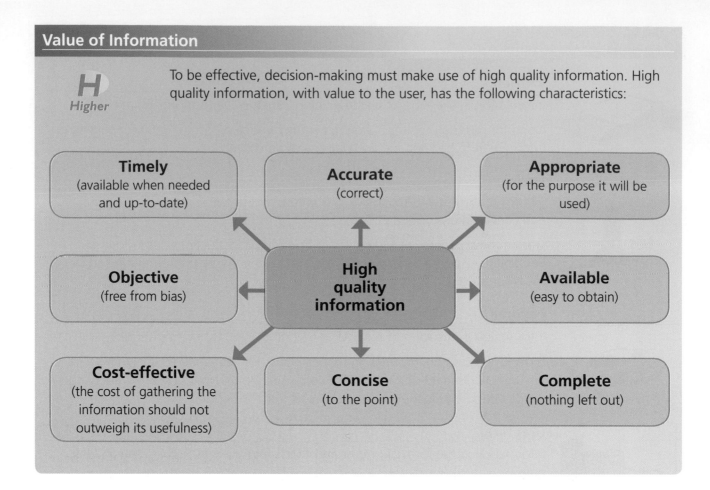

Higher

To be effective, decision-making must make use of high quality information. High quality information, with value to the user, has the following characteristics:

Timely
(available when needed and up-to-date)

Accurate
(correct)

Appropriate
(for the purpose it will be used)

Objective
(free from bias)

High quality information

Available
(easy to obtain)

Cost-effective
(the cost of gathering the information should not outweigh its usefulness)

Concise
(to the point)

Complete
(nothing left out)

Uses of Information in Business

The value of information also depends on the purpose for which it is used. Information is valuable if it:

Helps monitor and control the business
Information helps to ensure that the business is running smoothly and helps to check progress so that action can be taken if problems are highlighted. Internal information such as budgets and production/ sales records is especially useful.

Assists in decision-making
Owners and managers of a business have to make many decisions (including wage rates, product prices, suppliers and the number of people to hire) and they need accurate and up-to-date information to do this. Poor decision-making can have a serious negative impact on a business.

Measures performance
Owners and managers must evaluate how the business is performing financially (e.g. in meeting sales and production targets or using ratio analysis to allow comparisons to be made with previous years' or competitors' figures). Information must therefore be gathered to assist with this evaluation.

Identifies new business opportunities
Owners and managers must be aware of and collect information to identify any new or changing opportunities. They may want to collect written and oral information from primary and secondary sources to assist with this to ensure they continue to meet consumers' needs.

Networks

Local Area Networks (LANs) link up terminals on the same site and allow information to be shared to each terminal. One of the computers in the network is the fileserver that controls the hard disk containing the data files. Information that may be of interest to many users is held centrally. Users access the fileserver as required, avoiding the need for duplicate files.

A LAN can be linked via communication lines to become a WAN (Wide Area Network). Computers can be linked nationally and internationally.

Email

Each user has their own mailbox, similar to a postal address, on a computer. A user can check their box for mail and send messages to other computer mailboxes usually using the telephone line. Email has various advantages:

- it provides instant communication
- it can reach customers worldwide
- it is cost-effective as large numbers of mail items may be read, replied to, forwarded to other users, filed or deleted very quickly
- the same message may be sent to many users at the press of a key.

However, there has been an increase in the quantity of junk mail and staff may abuse the facility by sending personal mail which is costly in terms of staff time. Many computer viruses are spread via email.

Videoconferencing and webcams

This enables people in different locations to have meetings without the need to travel. A computer link is set up between people at two (or more) different locations, who can then meet via computer to speak to and see each other. Videoconferencing saves on travelling and accommodation costs. Less work time is lost through travelling.

However, connections can be poor or disrupted. If meetings are international then time differences can be a problem. There is a limit to the number of people who can effectively take part in a videoconference.

CASE STUDY

UHI Millenium Institute is a partnership between 15 different academic institutions in the north and west of Scotland stretching from Shetland to Dunoon and the Isle of Lewis to Perth. The partnership allows a much wider range of college and university level courses to be offered to students than one college alone could offer. The 15 institutions manage to do this through extensive use of videoconferencing.

Each college is equipped with approximately four videoconferencing suites. The system allows students in one location to have contact with a lecturer in another for lectures and tutorials. All 15 colleges can be linked together at the same time if required. In February 2006 there were 542 teaching videoconference links recorded between colleges.

The videoconference facilities are also used for administration and management meetings between sites.

Internet

The internet allows firms to access vast quantities of information via their computers such as government statistics, information about competitors and new products on the market. They can advertise their products on websites and use banking services.

However, it may be time-consuming to access suitable information due to the quantity available and there is no guarantee as to how up-to-date or accurate information is. Also, staff may use the internet unnecessarily so companies have to set up procedures to deal with staff who access inappropriate material.

E-commerce

Many businesses use their websites to sell their products and services to customers. Their products and services are displayed on their websites and customers can order online. This allows companies to sell products and services worldwide and internet-only businesses can cut costs by not having retail premises and large numbers of sales staff.

However, personal contact with customers is lost and many customers are still wary of purchasing over the internet.

CASE STUDY

E-commerce statistics

- Internet sales rose 81% between 2003 and 2004 to £71.1 billion.
- 98% of all large businesses have a website.
- The largest on-line sellers include the wholesale, retail, catering and travel businesses.
- On-line sales to businesses represent 75% of total on-line sales. Sales to private individuals only account for 25% of sales.

Adapted from Office of National Statistics

Interactive DVD

This is commonly used for staff training. It allows the user to control a video using a computer. The trainee watches the video and at certain points must decide what he/she would do next. The package responds in different ways according to how the trainee has answered.

Computer Aided Manufacture (CAM)

This is a type of technology used by manufacturers. It involves robots and computer-controlled machines in production. It saves on labour costs, produces consistent quality and does not stop for breaks or holidays! However, breakdowns can halt production and be very costly and time-consuming to fix.

Costs and Benefits of ICT

Benefits of ICT	Costs of ICT
Increases productivity.	Is costly due to cost of development, installation and maintenance, redundancy payments and retraining.
Reduces waste.	
Increases speed of work.	
Improves accuracy as computers tend to make fewer errors.	Can create problems (e.g. between workers and management when introducing technology).
Consistent production quality.	Requires new skills, often not manual, and staff retraining can often be difficult.
Saves labour.	
Increases access to information.	Causes stoppages in production and inconvenience when ICT breaks down.
Saves money as ICT is often less expensive and more reliable than labour.	
Saves floor space.	Can reduce level of staff motivation when workers are deskilled.
Improves communication and decision-making.	Data can be corrupted due to viruses, network faults or industrial espionage.
Improves working conditions as fewer accidents occur with new technology.	Technical support needs to be organised.

Business Software

Type of software

Databases

Used for keeping records of staff, customers and suppliers.

Functions of a database:

- Searches for specific information.
- Sorts records into order (e.g. alphabetical or numerical).
- Performs calculations within records (e.g. works out a supplier's balance).
- Produces reports which summarise the information (e.g. a sales manager can search a stock file to print out a list of all stock items which are not selling well).

Higher

The **Data Protection Act 1998** covers information that is held on computers. Businesses that keep individuals', staff's, suppliers' or customers' data on their computers must register with the Information Commissioner. They must state the purpose of holding the information. Individuals have the right of access to any information stored about them, can challenge it and claim compensation if information is inaccurate.

Companies which store information on individuals must:

- process information fairly and lawfully
- only hold information for a lawful purpose
- hold accurate information and keep it up-to-date
- not hold information for longer than necessary
- install security measures (e.g. use passwords) to prevent unauthorised, inappropriate access.

Type of software

Spreadsheet	This is an electronic worksheet that is used to calculate amounts. Functions of a spreadsheet: ● Performs calculations to provide, for example, totals, averages and ratios. ● Performs 'What if?' scenarios. By changing numbers in a spreadsheet the user can see the effect of this change on other figures. ● Produces charts or graphs of its calculations.
Word Processing (WP)	This makes the creation and editing of text easy and efficient. Key features of a word processor include: ● formatting commands (e.g. delete text, move and copy text, make bold, underline, use styles and sizes, spell-check, search and replace) ● mail-merge – a facility that allows information from a database to be merged into a WP document. (Mass-produced mail which arrives through your door with personal details on it has been produced using mail-merge.) ● importing and exporting text and graphics allows the user to incorporate into a document material produced on other software packages.
Desktop Publishing (DTP)	This is used to produce high quality, professional looking documents. DTP allows the user to import material produced on other packages and display text and graphics in a professional style.
Presentation packages	A business can make professional, well-displayed presentations where text, graphs, tables, graphics or organisation charts can be shown by a click of a mouse button. The computer can be linked to a data projector to display a presentation directly onto a large screen.
Computer Aided Design (CAD)	This software is used by architects, designers and engineers to design products in 3-D on computer. Changes to designs can be made easily without expensive redrawing by hand.

Uses of ICT

ICT is useful in an organisation because it:

- assists with effective decision-making
- assists with providing information for staff
- assists in maintaining accurate business records
- assists in effective communication within an organisation.

Effects of ICT

Effects on employees

- ICT results in greater productivity, therefore fewer staff will be required.
- Remaining staff may have to undertake retraining or updating of their skills to cope with the new technology – older staff may feel under pressure and may feel unable to cope with the changes.
- Relations with customers change with the introduction of ICT. The growth of e-commerce results in dealings with customers becoming more impersonal, since contact is increasingly made through online websites and telephone calls.
- Staff do not have the same personal contact with each other. Contact through emails is less personal than face-to-face meetings.
- Staff may take advantage of homeworking using ICT to communicate with colleagues.

Effects on organisations

- Introduction of ICT and improved communication can lead to decentralisation in a larger company with more decisions being made away from its head office. Email and videoconferencing assist with this.
- Additional departments may be created in the structure (e.g. an e-commerce department).
- As ICT results in fewer staff being required, redundancies and delayering may occur.
- As fewer staff are required, the span of control of managers may decrease.

○——— Quick Questions ———○

1 Identify and describe four sources of information.

2 Distinguish between quantitative and qualitative information.

3 Identify the characteristics that may influence the quality of information.

4 Information is valuable if it helps to measure business performance. Identify three other purposes information can be used for in a business.

5 Pick three types of ICT and state how each could be used within a large business.

6 Identify the advantages to a manufacturer introducing ICT in its production process.

7 Name the piece of legislation that governs information held about individuals on computer.

8 Pick three types of software and state how each could be used within a large business.

9 How might the introduction of ICT influence the employees of an organisation?

10 How might ICT affect the structure of an organisation?

Extended Response Questions

INTERMEDIATE 2

1 *Distinguish* between primary and secondary sources of information.

(3 marks)

2 *Name* and *describe* four types of information. *Suggest* an appropriate use an organisation could make of each type of information.

(12 marks)

> **Hint**
>
> If asked to 'distinguish' in a question use the word 'whereas' in each sentence, e.g. internal information comes from an organisation's own records whereas external information comes from outwith the organisation. Mention differences only.

3 A retailer can use email and the internet to promote and sell products to consumers. *Give* one advantage and one disadvantage of each in relation to promoting and selling products to consumers.

(4 marks)

4 *Identify* a software package that would be used within the Human Resources Department, *give* an example of what it could be used for and *outline* its main features.

(4 marks)

HIGHER

1 *Discuss* the costs and benefits of different sources of information. (12 marks)

2 A potential investor in a plc should access different types of information before making an investment decision. They may look at newspaper reports on the performance and share price of a company.
Discuss the value and reliability that this information may be to a potential investor.

(6 marks)

3 Dyson took a decision in 2002 to relocate its manufacturing operation of vacuum cleaners and washing machines to Malaysia but keep its Head Office in Wiltshire.
Describe the technology that the company may now use to communicate between Head Office and managers at the Malaysian factory. *Justify* the use of each technology chosen.

(6 marks)

4 A large factory would like to alter production to an automated CAM process.
Describe the effect that this may have on:
i) the employees
ii) the production process.

(6 marks)

> **Decision-making**   making a choice from different options.

Types of Decisions

Strategic decisions

Strategic decisions are long-term decisions made by senior managers. These decisions concern the organisation's strategic objectives (its overall purpose and direction). Strategic objectives often start with 'to improve …' (e.g. to improve profitability, to improve company image or to improve efficiency).

Tactical decisions

Tactical decisions are medium-term decisions. These decisions are about how to achieve the organisation's strategic objectives and are made by middle managers. For example, if an organisation's strategic objective is to improve profitability then a tactical decision may be to offer a redundancy package to staff to cut staffing costs.

Operational decisions

Operational decisions are short-term (day-to-day) decisions. All staff, regardless of level, may make operational decisions, although departmental/section managers may make more of these types of decisions when a change occurs (e.g. to call in a repair firm when equipment breaks down or to reorganise the shift rota when staff are ill).

Mission Statement

When senior management have decided on their strategic objectives they often let their staff, customers and suppliers know about these by producing a Mission Statement. This is a written summary of the objectives of the company, and is usually no more than one page long. It is often displayed in the organisation's reception area.

Decision-Making Process

Higher

Making a structured decision involves nine steps that can be remembered using **POGADSCIE**:

P   Identify the **P**roblem

O   Identify the **O**bjectives

G   **G**ather information

A   **A**nalyse the gathered information

D   **D**evise possible solutions

S   **S**elect the best solution

C   **C**ommunicate the decision

I   **I**mplement the decision

E   **E**valuate the effectiveness of the decision and the influence of ICT.

Illustration of POGADSCIE for a small clothes shop

Identify the problem	Sales have been falling for the last six months.
Identify the objective	To increase sales.
Gather information	Survey customers and staff about products. Gather information about competitors.
Analyse the gathered information	Look through all available information to work out reasons for fall in sales.
Devise possible solutions	Reduce sales prices. Have some local advertising. Change supplier to sell different stock.
Select the best solution	Change supplier and advertise.
Communicate the decision	Inform staff about changes to happen.
Implement the decision	Inform old supplier that they will no longer be used. Order new products. Launch advertising campaign.
Evaluate the effectiveness of the decision and the influence of ICT	Monitor customer responses to new stock and sales levels. Carry out market research to find out effectiveness of advertising.

Role of Managers in Decision-Making

One of the important skills a manager must possess is the ability to make good decisions, as managers have responsibility for the running of a business. Most decisions in an organisation will be taken by managers at department, middle or senior management level. Senior and middle managers tend to make strategic and tactical decisions whilst department/section managers tend to make more operational decisions. As managers make most decisions, organisational success depends very heavily on their ability to make the best decisions. Managers' decisions should be in line with the overall objectives of the organisation and use all available information. A good manager will ensure staff are kept informed of decisions made.

Influence of Stakeholders on Decision-Making

See **Stakeholders** (page 15).

SWOT Analysis

Higher

This is used in the first three steps of the decision-making process (i.e. in 'POG'). It involves identifying internal strengths and weaknesses (i.e. strengths and weaknesses within an organisation) and external opportunities and threats (i.e. opportunities and threats outside the organisation). It can be used to analyse a specific person's, product's or department's performance or any other aspect of an organisation.

Strengths	Internal areas or activities in which the organisation performs well.
Weaknesses	Internal areas or activities in which the organisation performs poorly.
Opportunities	External areas or activities that the organisation could profitably be involved with in the future.
Threats	External areas or activities of, for example, competitors; government policy; economic forces.

Conclusions with justifications should be drawn up from a SWOT to allow future action to be highlighted.

Internal areas which may be analysed as strengths or weaknesses	External areas which may be analysed as opportunities or threats
Sales and Marketing	Political situation
Human Resources (Staffing)	Economic climate
Organisational structure	Social or demographic changes
Operations and Production	Technological changes
Finance	Consumer tastes
Technology	Competitors
Management styles and structure	Suppliers
Products	Environmental changes

A SWOT analysis should be used to:

- identify and build on the business's strengths
- assist with the decision-making process. The strengths and weaknesses sections help with identifying the problem; the strengths, opportunities and threats sections help with identifying objectives; all sections help with gathering and analysing information
- correct any weaknesses identified
- take advantage of opportunities available
- provide measures to protect against threats or change threats into opportunities (e.g. people sharing MP3 files over the internet is viewed as a threat to music companies but these companies have now set up their own systems to provide a similar service, therefore turning a threat into a new opportunity to be exploited by them)
- make a firm proactive rather than reactive to changes in the business environment.

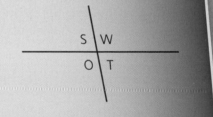

Hint

A SWOT analysis can be laid out as a list, table or diagram (as shown below). Bullet points are often used to list points under each heading.

Costs and Benefits of POGADSCIE and SWOT

Higher

Benefits	Costs
No rash decisions are made as time is taken to gather information and analyse the situation carefully.	Can be time-consuming to gather information and conduct analysis and could therefore slow down decision-making.
Decisions are made using relevant knowledge of facts and information that have been gathered.	Choosing from a range of possible solutions can often be very difficult to do in practice.
Time has been taken to develop alternative solutions rather than jumping to the first possible solution.	A structured process can stifle creativity and gut reactions to problems.
By following a logical process, ideas are enhanced because a range of alternative solutions will have been analysed.	

Why is Effective Decision-Making Difficult?

Higher

Internal constraints	External constraints
Finance may restrict an organisation's ability to choose the best solution.	Political factors (including government and EU laws).
Existing company policy may restrict an organisation's options.	Economic changes.
Staff may resist change.	Social factors.
A company may lack appropriate technology.	Technological development.
Decision-making staff may have tunnel vision, be unable to handle complex decisions, may fail to consult, or may be indecisive.	Environmental changes.
	Competitors' activities.

What do Quality Decisions Depend On?

Higher

- Having managers capable of making good decisions.
- The staff's ability to use decision-making techniques.
- The quantity and quality of information decision-makers have access to.
- The level of risk the decision-maker is willing to take.
- The personal interests the decision-maker may have.

Other Decision-Making Techniques

There are several other tools that can be used to help make an effective decision:

- **Brainstorming** – a group think of as many ideas as possible in a short period time. Each idea is then discussed fully to identify feasible solutions.
- **PEST analysis** – similar to a SWOT but Political, Economic, Social and Technological factors are identified. A business can then develop strategies to deal with each.

○ ———— Quick Questions ———— ○

1 Give a definition of a strategic, a tactical and an operational decision.
2 Give an example of each type of decision.
3 Explain what POGADSCIE means.
4 Why is it important that managers are able to make good decisions?
5 What is a SWOT analysis?
6 What are the advantages of using a POGADSCIE?
7 What are the disadvantages of preparing a SWOT Analysis?
8 What can happen within an organisation to make decision-making difficult?
9 What can happen outwith an organisation to make decision-making difficult?
10 What may influence the quality of the decisions a manager makes?

INTERMEDIATE 2

1 *Identify* and *describe* the three types of decision managers can make. *Give* an example of each. (9 marks)

2 *Suggest* two ways in which a manager can ensure effective decision-making takes place within an organisation. (2 marks)

HIGHER

1 News headline: POLICE TO MAKE SOCIETY SAFER.
This is an example of one type of decision a manager will make.
i) *Identify* and *describe* two other types of decisions an organisation could make. *Give* an example of each in relation to the police force. (6 marks)
ii) *Describe* the internal and external factors that may influence the effectiveness of the police force's decisions. (6 marks)

2 Effective decision-making is a vital characteristic of a good manager. *Outline* the techniques that a manager could use to ensure effective decisions are made. (8 marks)

3 *Discuss* the value of using decision-making techniques when making complex business decisions. (6 marks)

Hint
When asked to 'discuss' in a question mention advantages/reasons for and disadvantages/reasons against.

4 INTERNAL ORGANISATION

Internal organisation	the way in which an organisation may group its staff and work.

Types of Organisational Groupings

Grouping

Functional grouping

Functional groups are departments where staff have similar skills and expertise, and do similar jobs. An organisation which has functional grouping will typically have departments for Marketing, Finance, Human Resources, Operations and Research and Development.

✔ Advantages ✔	✘ Disadvantages ✘
■ Staff with similar expertise are kept together allowing specialisation. ■ Organisation has a clear structure. ■ Staff know who to turn to when they need a job done.	■ Organisation may become too large to be managed effectively. ■ It may be unresponsive to change. ■ Individual departments may become more concerned about their own interests rather than the organisation's strategic objectives.

Product/ service grouping

Higher

Product/service groups are divisions/departments where each deals with a different product or product range. For example, a TV company could have a Sports Division, a Film Division and a Music Division. Each division has its own functional staff.

✔ Advantages ✔	✘ Disadvantages ✘
■ Each division can be more responsive to changes in its field. ■ Expertise can develop within each division regarding its product/service. ■ Can give more incentive for staff to perform better. ■ Management can more easily identify the parts of a business that are doing well and those that are not.	■ There may be unnecessary duplication of resources/tasks/personnel across different products. ■ Divisions may find themselves competing with one another.

Customer grouping

Higher

Customer groups are divisions dealing with different types of customer. There may be a different division for Retail, for Trade, for Overseas and for Mail Order Customers.

✔ Advantages ✔	✘ Disadvantages ✘
■ Each division is able to give a service, price and promotions suited to its own type of customer. ■ Customer loyalty builds up because of personal service.	■ This method of grouping can be more expensive because of greater staff costs. Additional staff have to be employed to deal with a new customer grouping (e.g. if an e-commerce division was to be created). ■ Possible duplication of administration, finance and marketing procedures.

CASE STUDY

Arnold Clark Organisation Chart

Arnold Clark has functional departments for Finance, Administration and Operations. It has different departments for different types of products it offers, e.g. Car Rental and Sales. It also has two departments that are divided according to customer grouping. One department targets corporate and private customers and another for major accounts such as local authorities.

It is unlikely that a large organisation has only one type of grouping.

Chart adapted from www.arnoldclarkfinance.co.uk

Place/territory grouping

Higher

Staff are divided into divisions, each dealing with a different geographical area. A place/territory organisation may have a Scottish Division, a North of England Division, a Midlands Division, a South-East Division and a South-West Division, for example.

✔ Advantages ✔	✘ Disadvantages ✘
■ It allows an organisation to cater for the needs of customers in different geographical locations.	■ It can be expensive to staff, with administration, finance and marketing procedures duplicated in various divisions.

Technology grouping

Higher

This is a grouping in which a manufacturing company groups its business activities according to technological or production processes. This type of grouping is only suitable for large organisations which have different products and production processes.

Line/staff grouping Higher	This is a grouping in which the organisation is divided up into line departments involved in generating revenue (i.e. Sales), and staff departments providing specialist support for the whole organisation (e.g. Finance and Human Resources).

A business may use more than one type of grouping to organise its activities. A multinational company may use place/territory groupings by having a US Division, a European Division and a Far East Division. Each division may be split into functional groupings with each territory having its own Marketing Department, Finance Department, HR Department and Operations Department.

Organisation Charts

An organisation chart is a diagram that shows the formal structure of an organisation. An organisation chart shows:

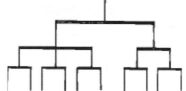

- the relationships between staff
- who has authority over whom
- who is in charge of the organisation and each department
- the chain of command and lines of communication.

Chain of command

This shows the way authority and instructions are passed down vertically through an organisation. If the chain of command is long then decision-making and communication may be slow.

CASE STUDY

Chain of command in the Scottish Police Force

Chief Constable
↓
Deputy Chief Constable
↓
Assistant Chief Constable
↓
Chief Superintendent
↓
Superintendent
↓
Chief Inspector
↓
Inspector
↓
Sergeant
↓
Constable

Taken from www.police-information.co.uk

Span of control

This means the number of subordinates working under a superior or manager. A reasonable span of control is from four to seven staff. The span of control depends on: the capability of the manager; the capability of the subordinates; the task being undertaken; and the procedures that operate in the organisation. A tall hierarchy gives a narrow span of control and a flat structure gives a wide span of control.

A narrow span

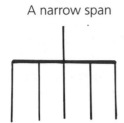

A wide span

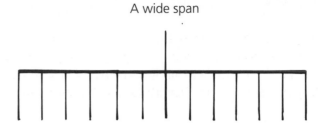

A narrow span means:

- the manager is able to supervise staff closely, which may put staff under greater pressure
- a manager may not have enough staff to share ideas with
- subordinates may barely have time to complete a task before the manager gives them the next
- there is a danger of interference by the manager.

A wide span means:

- a high degree of delegation is required which needs a high quality of staff
- there may be queues for the manager's time leading to delays in decision-making
- a manager will be under pressure to deal with everyone swiftly – snap judgements or poor quality decisions may be made
- subordinates may be forced to make decisions themselves when matters cannot wait for the manager and the manager may lose control
- the manager will have less time for planning.

Formal Organisational Structure

There are various factors which affect the formal structure of an organisation. These include:

- the size of the organisation – the larger an organisation becomes the more formal its structure may be. With more staff and departments there is greater need for structure and control
- the technology used within the organisation – introduction of e-commerce by an organisation may result in a new department being created thereby affecting its structure. As new technologies are introduced it may result in staff redundancies or downsizing
- the market in which the organisation operates – if an organisation operates on a national level it may be more formal as it is likely to be a larger organisation. Smaller, local organisations may be less formally structured
- the staff skills within the organisation – if staff are highly skilled in an organisation then more independence may be given to staff resulting in a flat, decentralised structure
- the products or services made or supplied by the organisation – if an organisation produces many products or services there may be more departments resulting in a larger more formal organisation.

> **Hint**
>
> Include any relevant diagrams in organisational structure questions. Remember to label your diagrams.

Organisations can be structured in the following ways:

Type of structure	
Hierarchical 	A traditional organisational structure with the organisation chart looking like a tall pyramid with many management levels. Decisions and instructions are passed down from senior staff with information passing back up. Employees tend to be specialised in departments and know their levels of responsibility and roles. Communication may be slow, resulting in resistance to change and inflexibility.
Flat 	This is a low pyramid with few management levels. Information can be easily passed between levels. There are few levels of management and a short chain of command, giving more independence to each department. This structure suits small- and medium-sized organisations.
Entrepreneurial	Small businesses use this structure. Decisions are made by a few people at the core of the organisation. Decisions can be made quickly; staff know who they are accountable to and the decision-maker does not need to consult staff. This structure is difficult to use in a larger business and can create a heavy workload for the few decision-makers. It can also stifle initiative from other staff. Higher
Matrix 	A matrix structure can often be set up for part of an organisation when needed. A project team is created to carry out a specific task. Team members come from different functional areas. Higher

A project team might be set up to develop a new product, launch a new service or introduce a new IT system. Each team would have a specialist in marketing, finance, operations and R&D. Each specialist would report to the project manager as well as their normal functional manager.

The benefits of this structure include increased experience, motivation and job satisfaction as staff can use their particular expertise in different situations. It is good for tackling complex problems. However, it can be costly to have a variety of different teams. It may be difficult to co-ordinate a team with staff from different functional areas. There can also be confusion as to who reports to whom as each specialist reports to two managers. |
| **Decentralised** 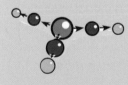 | Control and decision-making is delegated to departments, which relieves senior management from routine day-to-day tasks and burdens. As subordinates are given responsibility, they are motivated and decision-making is quicker. This structure could be used, for example, by a retail chain with different stores. Each store manager would be responsible for the running and decision-making within her or his own store allowing them to use local knowledge of consumers and the market in their decision-making. |
| **Centralised** | Control and decision-making lies with top management in head office. Top management are more likely to possess high quality decision-making skills. This is often seen in a hierarchical structure. Procedures can be standardised for purchasing and hiring, for example. Decisions can be made for the whole organisation. It is also easier to promote a corporate image when procedures are standardised. However, staff who do not make the decisions have very little authority or room for initiative. Decisions made may not reflect local conditions. |

A typical hairdressers salon will have a flat structure.

Compare this with the organisational structure of the Scottish Police force that has nine different levels.

```
        Owner/top stylist
    ┌─────────┼─────────┐
  Stylist   Stylist   Stylist
              │
            Junior
```

The Role and Responsibility of Management

It is the responsibility of management to ensure:

- the most appropriate formal structure is developed
- staff are made aware of the structure and their place in the organisation
- that informal structures and relationships are allowed to develop
- changes to the structure are made only when necessary, i.e. when introducing online shopping an e-commerce department may be created. Unnecessary or too frequent changes in structure may only confuse staff and customers.

Organisational Relationships

Line relationship

This exists between a manager and her/his subordinate(s). It is a vertical relationship in which work is allocated from the manager to her/his subordinate(s). The manager has authority over her/his subordinate(s).

Lateral relationship

This exists between staff on the same horizontal level of the organisation.

Functional relationship

This exists where a specialist function is given to a department (e.g. Human Resources); that department is given responsibility for the function throughout the organisation. For example, a Human Resources department has a functional relationship with all the other departments in the organisation.

Staff relationship

This is where someone (e.g. a computer consultant) has an advisory relationship with another member of staff. He/she has no authority over departments as he/she only advises.

Informal relationship

These can develop between staff at breaks, during work and when socialising. This builds up a range of sources staff can seek advice from. Staff share information with each other and communicate regarding work-related (and non-work related!) matters. All organisations have informal relationships within them.

A line relationship exists between the Store Manager and the Food Section, Textiles and Retail Operations Managers. They in turn have a line relationship with their department staff.

A lateral relationship exists between the Food Section, Textiles and Retail Operations Managers. All bottom level staff have a lateral relationship with each other.

Sample organisation chart of a small Marks & Spencer store

Changes in Organisational Structure

Type of change

Delayering

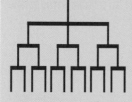

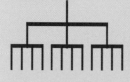

This involves reducing staff levels by cutting out levels of management to flatten the structure. This creates a smaller hierarchy where each manager has an increased span of control. Delayering helps to:

- improve communication
- make decision-making quicker and more effective
- empower staff
- cut costs as there are fewer management salaries to pay
- allow an organisation to respond more quickly to market changes.

Delayering leads to more responsibility and a wider span of control for the remaining managers. However, delayering also causes redundancies as well as giving fewer promotion opportunities for remaining staff.

Downsizing

This involves removing certain areas of the organisation's activities by closing factories or merging divisions together. A business may downsize then outsource some functions, i.e. delivery. *See* Methods of Growth (page 24) for more details on outsourcing. Downsizing helps to:

- cut costs and increase profits
- empower remaining staff
- become more competitive and efficient.

However, downsizing may lead to a company losing valuable skills, experience and knowledge of many staff resulting in low staff morale during the downsizing process.

Empowerment

Higher

Empowerment means giving staff responsibility for their own work and decision-making by delegation, transfer of responsibility and greater access to information. This often occurs when a business delayers or downsizes.

Empowering staff may lead to:
- employees being more motivated and productive (as their work is not being checked)
- increased pay and training for staff
- enhanced promotion prospects
- decisions being made by the people who do the work, and so decision-making is quicker
- staff developing greater skills
- the organisation becoming more streamlined.

An organisation benefits from empowerment by having:
- good decisions taken quickly
- staff being more flexible and motivated
- improved productivity
- improved competitiveness
- more ideas on how to solve problems
- improved communication as fewer managers are required.

Empowerment may not be successful because:
- not all staff may want to be involved in decision-making
- managers may be unwilling to give up some responsibility for decision-making
- empowerment may come after delayering or downsizing. Therefore remaining staff may not trust the organisation.
- it can be costly to train staff to make appropriate decisions.

Corporate Culture

Higher

Corporate culture	is the values, beliefs and norms relating to the company or organisation that are shared by all its staff.

Corporate culture is developed through:
- the ideals and principles of the founder, owners or senior management
- the use of symbols, logos, mottoes, uniforms, shop layouts and examples of outstanding employees.

Communication of corporate culture
Staff have to be made aware of the corporate culture. This can, for example, be done through: honouring employees for excellent work, training courses, company magazines/newsletters, company events, social events, staff uniforms and company videos.

Advantages of strong corporate culture
- Employees feel part of the organisation.
- Increased staff motivation.
- Improved employee relationships.
- Increased employee loyalty.
- Increased productivity.

1 Describe the terms 'product grouping' and 'place grouping'.
2 What are the advantages and disadvantages of customer grouping?
3 Describe how a business can use several different types of structural groupings.
4 What is the purpose of an organisation chart?
5 What are the disadvantages of a wide span of control?
6 Describe the factors that affect the formal structure of an organisation.
7 When would a matrix structure be used by an organisation?
8 Describe three relationships that can exist in an organisation.
9 Why might an organisation delayer?
10 Why might an organisation empower staff?

Extended Response Questions

INTERMEDIATE 2

1 *Describe* each of the following: span of control, functional organisation, downsizing, informal relationships. (4 marks)

2 *Distinguish* between a tall and a flat structure. (6 marks)

3 Many organisations have had to restructure in recent years. *Suggest* two ways in which an organisation can restructure. *Describe* the effect each could have on an organisation. (6 marks)

HIGHER

1 Standard Life is a company selling financial services. They have sales representatives covering different areas of Scotland.
i) *Identify* the type of organisational grouping that is described for Standard Life. *Justify* your choice. (2 marks)
ii) *Discuss* two other ways that Standard Life could group its activities. (8 marks)

2 Hairdresser businesses often have a flat structure with a wide span of control. *Describe* why this is and *describe* the advantages of this for the owner. (6 marks)

3 *Discuss* the implications for a business moving to decentralised decision-making. (6 marks)

4 *Explain* how an organisation might benefit from empowering its employees. (5 marks)

Hint
Remember to check what the command words in each question means on page 6.

| *Marketing* | the anticipation, identification and fulfilment of customer needs |

The Role and Importance of Marketing

The purpose of marketing is to:

- help to raise awareness of products and services on offer
- help to raise the organisation's profile in the market
- encourage customers to purchase
- target new customers and retain existing ones
- allow an organisation to know what customers want
- assist with monitoring changing tastes and trends in the market
- allow an organisation to meet its strategic objectives which could include:
  to increase or maximise profits
  to increase market share (the market portion held by a business or by an individual brand)
  to extend the life of a current brand
  to become the market leader
  to increase the product portfolio.

Different types of organisations have different strategic objectives, which marketing helps to achieve. For example:

- a local authority may want to increase public use of certain facilities
- a charity may want to increase donations or raise awareness of the plight of others
- the police may want to raise awareness of certain campaigns and reduce crime figures
- a private sector business may want to increase profitability by making customers aware of new products or services being sold.

CASE STUDY

The grocery market in Scotland is worth an estimated £10 billion. Tesco is well established as the market leader with a share of approximately 31% of the market. Asda has a 21% share of the market and Morrisons has 12%.

Adapted from *Daily Express* article on Saturday 8 April 2006

External Factors

Organisations (including their Marketing departments) must take account of the environment in which they operate. This environment is made up of 'external factors', so called because they are outside the organisation's control. They include:

> **P**olitical factors
> **E**conomic factors
> **S**ocial factors
> **T**echnological factors
> **E**nvironmental factors
> **C**ompetitive factors.

Product orientation/product led

This is an approach to business where a company first manufactures a product and then tries to persuade customers to purchase it. The company does not conduct any market research before production commences. Product research and product testing are key elements in a product led business.

Market orientation/market led

This is an approach to business which puts customers' needs at the centre of the company's decision-making process. Market research and market testing are key elements in a market led organisation.

The advantages for a company in adopting a market orientation approach include:

- it is more likely to produce products that customers want
- it will be more able to anticipate and meet changes in customer demands
- it will be able to make changes to its products or develop new products easily as it listens to customers.

Customer and Industrial Markets

Customer markets are made up of individuals who purchase goods and/or services, usually from retailers, for their personal use.

Industrial markets are made up of organisations that purchase goods and/or services from other organisations to help them produce their own goods and/or services. These organisations are either manufacturers (e.g. soft drink makers) or service companies (e.g. banks and insurance companies).

Market Segmentation

This involves splitting customers into different groups. Customers can be grouped in many ways, including by:

- socio-economic group (e.g. A, B, C1, C2, D and E)
- family lifestyle
- age
- religion
- occupation
- income
- gender
- geographical location.

The following social classes are used by the advertising and market research industries. Each household is usually graded according to occupation/employment status of the main income earner.

A Very senior managers or professionals, top civil servants.

B Middle managers in large organisations, principal officers in local government, top managers/owners of small businesses.

C1 Junior managers, owners of small businesses, other non-manual workers.

C2 Skilled manual workers.

D Semi-skilled and un-skilled workers, apprentices.

E People on long term benefits and casual workers.

Market segmentation is useful to an organisation as it can assist with:

- developing **products** that are appropriate to customers and highlighting gaps in the market
- setting appropriate **prices**
- ensuring that products are sold in the appropriate **places** for the target customers
- ensuring that appropriate **promotions** are offered to the target customers.

Niche marketing

Companies sometimes identify a niche (gap) in a certain market. This involves aiming a product at a small market segment. The Whisky Shop, Saga and Aston Martin take advantage of niche marketing. Niche marketing is popular as it allows businesses to:

- build up expertise in one type of product and customer
- avoid competition as niches are often not considered profitable by larger organisations.

However, companies which identify a niche and achieve significant market growth* often attract competition. They also have a high risk of failure as they rely on a small group of customers.

* Market growth is the rate at which the whole market area increases. It is often expressed as a percentage. For example, if the tourist industry in the UK experiences a market growth of 10% per annum this year, 10% more sales revenue will be generated from tourists this year in the UK compared to last year.

HBOS (Halifax and the Bank of Scotland) divide customers into groups by product they should be targeted with. They allocate like-minded customers to groups then target each group with promotions and products they believe the group will be interested in. Each group may consist of different ages, geographical locations, etc. There may be a group that they target with information about mortgage products and another that they target with savings products. As information gets updated customers may move from one group to another as their financial requirements alter.

HBOS also do a small amount of traditional market segmentation by age and lifestyle. This allows them to identify gaps in the marketplace. A few of the groups they have identified are:

YOUTH   Pre-university, University and Post-University – targeted with loans and student banking facilities.

AFFLUENTS   Customers with a high net worth can be targeted with private banking facilities.

Differentiated and Undifferentiated Marketing

Higher

Differentiated marketing involves providing different products and services for particular market segments. For example, some car manufacturers produce different cars for different customers – the Ford Ka is aimed at young, single, cost-conscious customers, whereas the Ford Focus is aimed at customers aged 25–35 who may have young children.

Undifferentiated marketing involves aiming products and services at the population as a whole without producing different products for different market segments. For example, Heinz uses undifferentiated marketing as most of its products are targeted at the majority of the population. It does not produce one type of baked beans for AB customers and another for CD customers.

Market Research

Market research	the systematic gathering, recording and analysing of data about an organisation's products and/or services and its target market.

Market research allows a firm to:

- anticipate changes in the market and customer tastes
- keep ahead of competitors
- ensure their product/service meets customer requirements
- ensure the correct price and promotions are set
- ensure the product/service is sold in the most appropriate places
- attract new market segments.

Market research can provide an organisation with information about:

- the size and nature of its target market
- the age, sex, income level and preferences of customers
- the effectiveness of its selling methods
- what customers think of its products and prices
- the effectiveness of its advertising and promotions
- a test product and how it can be improved.

Information gathered must be analysed correctly to be of value. The sample used must be of sufficient size to be representative of the market/population. The actual survey or questionnaire must be constructed and used correctly.

The two market research methods

Desk research is carried out by a researcher using secondary information in the form of published sources (e.g. government reports, trade journals, financial papers, profit and loss accounts) originally produced by someone other than the researcher. (For strengths and weaknesses *see* **Sources of Information**, **Secondary Information**, page 30.)

Field research is carried out by a researcher 'in the field' in order to obtain first-hand information for an organisation to use. The researcher goes out to the market and obtains the information her/himself. (For strengths and weaknesses *see* **Sources of Information**, **Primary Information**, page 30.)

Most field research techniques involve the use of a questionnaire, survey or an interview to gather information.

Field research technique	✔ Advantages ✔	✘ Disadvantages ✘
Personal interview involves a face-to-face interview. A personal interview can be held in the street or home (street responses are more brief, less friendly and less detailed than home interviews).	■ Allows two-way communication ■ The researcher can encourage the respondent to answer. ■ Mistakes and misunderstandings made during an interview can be dealt with immediately.	■ Personal interviews can be expensive as researchers have to be selected and trained. ■ Home interviews tend to be unpopluar with consumers.
Focus group/group discussions involves specially selected groups of people. It is usually led by an experienced chairperson who puts forward points to encourage open discussion.	■ Qualitative information in the form of opinions, feelings and attitudes are gained.	■ Can be difficult to analyse qualitative information.
Telephone survey involves a market researcher telephoning people at home and asking them questions.	■ Relatively inexpensive. ■ The response is immediate. ■ A large number of people can be surveyed quickly.	■ Many people do not like strangers asking questions over the phone, therefore hostility can be encountered.
Postal survey involves a market researcher sending a questionnaire out through the post.	■ Inexpensive as it does not require a trained interviewer.	■ Questions must be simple and easy to answer. ■ The response rate is very low. Consequently, incentives are often offered to fill in and return the questionnaire (e.g. free gifts or entry to a prize draw).
Consumer audit is used by large market research organisations to carry out continuous research to monitor, for example, the buying habits of customers, influence of advertising and effect of price changes. Certain customers are issued with a diary and asked to record some or all of their purchases which are then monitored by the market research company.	■ Accurate information can be gained if the diaries are kept properly. ■ Information can indicate customer trends as they are completed over a period of time.	■ This is an expensive method to use as participants receive payment. ■ There is a high turnover of respondents as filling the diaries in can be regarded as a nuisance. ■ Diaries may be inaccurate or incomplete.

Field research technique	✔ Advantages ✔	✘ Disadvantages ✘
Hall test involves inviting customers to look at and/or try a product and then give their reactions to it. Often used by supermarkets when trialling new products.	■ Information gained is qualitative.	■ Can be difficult to analyse qualitative information. ■ Results can be flawed because testers feel obliged to make complimentary comments about a product.

CASE STUDY

Mackie's Limited are located near Inverurie in the North East of Scotland. Mackie's has 11% of the premium ice-cream market in the UK and are the brand leaders in Scotland. To gather information about existing and new products they use a taste panel/hall test made up staff volunteers selected by passing tests which prove a high sensitivity for flavours and aromas. The panel aim to:

● assess objectively all products to ensure that Mackie's ice cream quality remains consistent

● compare Mackies ice cream with competitors, to maintain and understand its uniqueness

● describe objectively what customers like best as identified through consumer product testing

● test new products – carry out likeability tests and provide a first response to new product ideas.

Adapted from www.mackies.co.uk

EPOS (Electronic Point of Sale) is used by retailers when Switch/loyalty cards are swiped through their electronic tills. Information about individual customers' shopping habits are recorded by the computerised tills.	■ Can give very accurate customer profiles. ■ Allows retailers to offer promotions that are tailored to customers' needs. ■ Assists with monitoring brand loyalty and the effect of price changes.	■ Can be very expensive to set up the system to record consumer spending.
Observation involves a person being allocated the task of watching and recording particular occurrences or habits (e.g. recording the number of cars which pass a certain point on the road at a particular time to measure road usage and congestion).	■ Provides accurate quantitative information.	■ Cannot ask questions that explain customers actions as there is no direct contact with customers.
Test marketing involves launching a new product in a regional area only. Reaction to the new product is monitored and if the product is successful in the test market, it may then be launched worldwide.	■ It may highlight particular aspects of the product that customers dislike. These aspects can be amended before a national launch. ■ Saves an expensive national launch if the product fails in the test area.	■ Customers in one area may have regional tastes that are not representative of the national population.

Sampling

When conducting market research it is often not feasible to question every potential respondent. A sample of respondents has to be selected. They can be selected by various means:

Random sampling

Individuals are pre-selected from a list, perhaps the telephone directory or electoral register. The interviewer makes a number of calls to randomly chosen people from the list. It is expensive to operate as the people who have been selected must be interviewed – if they are not in, the interviewer must return at another time to obtain their responses. This limits bias being introduced, but a large sample is required if the sample is to be representative of the whole population.

Higher

Stratified random sampling

This makes a random group more representative of the population as a whole. The sample is divided up into segments based on how the population is divided up. For example, if the researcher knows that 10% of the population are in socio-economic group AB, 50% in C and 40% in DE, he/she will ensure that 10% of the sample are selected from the AB group, 50% from the C group and 40% of respondents from the DE group.

Quota sampling

The researcher is given instructions as to the number of people to interview and their characteristics (e.g. age, sex, marital status and income group). It is the job of the researcher to find and interview the people who fit the categories required. This is cheaper than random sampling.

Structure of a Questionnaire

Most market research methods use questionnaires. The aim of a questionnaire is to obtain meaningful answers from a large group of people. It should be short, simple and easy to understand. A good questionnaire must:

- have its purpose stated clearly
- have an easy-to-use layout
- have questions which are relevant to the purpose of the survey
- not rely too much on the respondent's memory
- be short, to the point and relevant to the subject
- start with a few easy questions to find out if the respondent is suitable
- avoid jargon, unfamiliar words and difficult concepts
- have questions in a logical order.

The Marketing Mix (The Four Ps)

Product   The goods/service that the customer purchases. The product includes the packaging, image, guarantee and after-sales service (i.e. the total offer).

Price   The actual amount paid for the product/service by the customer to the seller.

Place   Where the customer purchases the product/service.

Promotion   The way in which a customer is made aware of a product/service and is persuaded to buy it. Promotion includes advertising, sales promotions, exhibitions and personal (face-to-face) selling.

Product

Product	the actual item that a customer purchases, including the packaging, image, guarantee and after-sales service.

Product Life-Cycle

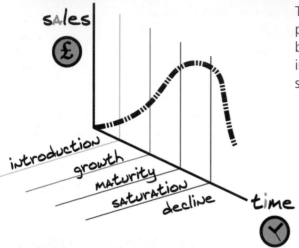

The product life-cycle shows the different stages a new product passes through over time and the sales that can be expected at each stage. There are generally five stages in any product life-cycle: introduction, growth, maturity, saturation and decline.

> ### Hint
> Include any relevant diagrams in product life-cycle or product mix questions. Remember to label your diagrams.

Introduction

The product is launched on the market. The costs of holding stock, advertising and promoting the product may be high at this stage. If the product is innovative, it will have few competitors and usually a high price.

Growth

Sales increase significantly as customer knowledge of the product increases. A few competitors launch their own versions of the product.

Maturity

The product becomes commonplace in the market. Growth begins to slow down. Competition increases and the price of the product falls.

Saturation

Competition becomes fierce and prices tumble. Customer tastes may begin to change. Not all competing products survive in this fiercely competitive environment.

Decline

Customer tastes change, technology changes and other new, more advanced products are launched. Sales fall, prices become very low and eventually the product is withdrawn from the market.

Some products, for example Mars, Persil, Heinz Baked Beans and Coca Cola, appear to never reach the decline stage. This is due to their having used successful extension strategies, constant brand promotion, having established strong brand loyalty over the years, having no close rivals and having established a high status in the market.

The length of the product life-cycle depends on the product. Car models have a life-cycle of approximately five years; latest clothes fashions often have a life-cycle of a few months; and CD singles tend to have a life-cycle of a few weeks.

Extension strategies

To stop a product from entering the decline phase, companies often try some of the following extension strategies to prolong the life of the product:

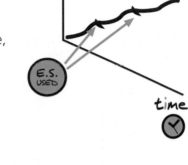

- **Improve the product.** Washing powder manufacturers often produce new, improved versions of their products.
- **Change the packaging** to appeal to a different market segment.
- **Change the channel of distribution.** For example, the introduction of internet shopping.
- **Change product prices.**
- **Change the promotional activities.**
- **Change the use customers have for the product.**
- **Rebrand the name of the product.** A name change can generate considerable publicity and new appeal. For example, the chocolate bar Marathon was changed to Snickers, Opal Fruits to Starburst and Dixons shops were changed to Currys.digital.
- **Produce line extensions.** For example, Coca Cola also produces Diet Coke, Cherry Coke and Caffeine-Free Coca Cola, which are all variations of the original product.

CASE STUDY

Lucozade was first produced in 1927. From its introduction until 1980 it was sold as a drink suitable for those who were ill or recovering from illness. 1985 first saw Lucozade being marketed as an energy drink to replace lost energy and adverts featured sportsman, Daley Thompson. This represented the shift in Lucozade from being marketed as a drink associated with ill health to one whose use was as a sports energy replacement drink.

Adapted from www.lucozade.co.uk *and* www.gsk.com

Product Mix and Branding

Term	Description
Product mix/ product portfolio 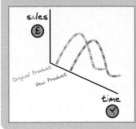	A firm's product mix or product portfolio is the range of products that it produces. Baxters Food Group have a product portfolio which includes jams, sauces, pickles and soups. By identifying the stage in the life-cycle of each of their products, a business can plan when to introduce new products as old products go into decline.
	Most firms have a range of products in order to spread risks. If a firm only produced one product and it failed, the firm itself would fail. A wide range of products can meet the needs of different market segments, increase profits, and raise the profile of the firm to become the market leader.

Term	Description
Product mix/ product portfolio cont'd *Higher*	Some firms use the Boston Matrix to analyse their product mix. The Boston Matrix is used to place the products a firm produces into one of four categories:

		Market share	
		High	Low
Market growth	High	⭐ Star	👤 Problem Child
	Low	🐄 Cash Cow	🐕 Dog

Companies should identify which of their products is in each category and then plan their marketing accordingly. For example, today's stars may end up being tomorrow's problem children or dogs, depending on the company's marketing activities.

CASE STUDY

Unilever is a large multinational organisation that manufactures approximately 400 brands worldwide in its product portfolio. In the UK there are approximately 40 Unilever brands including Persil, Domestos, Birds Eye, Lynx, Knorr and Slim-Fast.

Term	Description
Product line	The product mix may contain product lines. These are groups of products that are similar. For example, Procter & Gamble manufacture a hair care product line that includes Pantene, Herbal Essences and Head & Shoulders. They also have product lines for washing powders, cosmetics and household cleaners, amongst others.
Branding 	A brand is a name, symbol, design or combination of these given to a product or products by the producer which is intended to identify the goods produced. A brand may relate to an individual product (e.g. Irn-Bru), or a whole company (e.g. Heinz). Some brands are so powerful that they are in everyday use to describe a product, such as Hoover, Tippex and Sellotape.
	A manufacturer of a successful brand can save money on marketing, higher prices can be charged and customers may become brand loyal. It also becomes easier to launch new products with the same brand name.
	Brands often require a high level of advertising and research and development costs to maintain a high public profile. Some brands (especially clothing and accessories) are susceptible to being copied/faked which is expensive to fight against. A poor brand may affect the whole range of products produced by the one manufacturer.
	A customer may see a brand as a guarantee of high quality. A brand is easily recognisable. There may be 'snob value' in a customer using certain brands. However, some brands cost more as customers are paying for the expensive packaging and advertising.
Own labels/own brands	An own label/own brand refers to a retailer's own product which may be the retailer's own name such as Tesco Value or an exclusive brand to that retailer such as George at ASDA. The retailer does not normally produce the actual product.
	Own label products tend to need little advertising. Own label goods tend to be less expensive than other branded products but may be seen to be of inferior quality.

Top Scottish brands associated with Scotland	UK's top favourite online brands
1 Irn Bru	1 Google
2 Tennants	2 bbc.co.uk
3 Baxters	3 eBay
4 Glenmorangie	4 Streetmap
5 = Bank of Scotland	5 Friends Reunited
5 = Famous Grouse	6 Nectar
5 = Scottish Widows	7 Tiscali
8 = Standard Life	8 Times Online
8 = Tunnocks	9 Topshop
9 Visit Scotland	10 Yell.com

Adapted from www.mad.co.uk   *Adapted from www.bbc.co.uk/UGov*

Quick Questions

1 Why is marketing important to an organisation?
2 Name four ways that customers can be grouped for marketing purposes.
3 Describe the following terms: differentiated and undifferentiated marketing.
4 Name and give a definition of four different field research techniques.
5 Why is sampling necessary?
6 What is the marketing mix?
7 Draw and label the product life cycle of a product of your choice.
8 What strategies can a business use to prolong the life of a product?
9 Why should a business not rely on just one product?
10 What is a brand and an own-label?

Price

Price	the actual amount paid for the product/service by the customer to the seller.

Pricing decisions are especially important at certain times, for example when introducing new products, when the product life-cycle is to be extended, when placing existing products into a new market and during periods of rising costs. Pricing decisions are also made when competitors change their prices, when competitors alter other aspects of their marketing mix and when balancing prices between individual products in a product line.

Overall, the price a company charges for a product should be based on what the customer is prepared to pay for it. This is dependent on:

● the company's objectives
● competitors' prices
● the position of the product in its life-cycle

- the cost of manufacturing the product
- the time of year – if the company offers summer/Christmas sales or if the product is seasonal
- the level of advertising or other promotion
- the profit level expected
- suppliers' prices
- the market segment the product is aimed at
- the place where the product is sold
- the state of the economy (e.g. in a recession prices may fall)
- government pressure (e.g. car manufacturers reduced some prices following government pressure).

Pricing Strategies

Strategy	Description
Penetration pricing	This strategy is used by a company that wants to enter a market in which competitors already sell similar products. The company will initially set a price for its product lower than its competitors' to tempt customers to choose to buy its product rather than its competitors'. Once its product becomes popular with customers, its price is raised to be in line with competitors' prices.
Destroyer pricing	This is used by a company that wants to eliminate competition. Prices are lowered to force competitors' prices down. Weaker competition will be unable to survive and may be forced to leave the market. Prices then return to their original or higher level. This strategy can only be used by large companies who can afford to make losses until the competition has been eliminated.
Promotional pricing	Prices are reduced for a short period of time. This strategy is used by a company that wants to inject new life into a product or reduce stock levels quickly.
Premium pricing	High prices are set for a product or service and this high price is maintained to create an exclusive image for the product, e.g. Ferrari, Gucci, Timberland.
Loss leaders	Retailers often advertise a limited range of products at low, unprofitable prices in order to entice customers into their store. Once the customer is in the store, however, they will often buy other normally priced products and so the store will still make a profit from the customer's total purchases.
Competitive pricing	Some firms in the same market charge similar prices for products to avoid a price war. Some petrol companies, for example, do this. Instead of competing on price, firms use non-pricing factors such as advertising, promotions, packaging, etc.

Strategy	Description
Price discrimination	Some companies charge different prices for the same product according to the time of day, year or amount of usage. For example, BT charges different prices for a telephone call at different times of the day. Holiday firms charge different prices for the same holiday according to the time of year.
Market skimming	This happens when a company launches a new product at a high price. The high initial price allows a company to make a large initial profit and recoup some of the research and design costs before competitors enter the market. As competition increases, the price will gradually fall. New home entertainment electrical products tend to be introduced onto the market using market skimming pricing.

CASE STUDY

The bottled water market is very competitive. Prices have fallen greatly over the last 10 to 15 years. In the 1980s only high earners drank bottled water, there were few competitors which led to high prices being charged and high profits for manufacturers.

Nowadays bottled water is an everyday product. UK sales have grown from 350 million litres per year to 2 billion since the 1980s. Consumers now look for value for money and low prices.

Adapted from Scotland on Sunday article on 23/4/06 (www.scotlandonsunday.scotsman.com)

Calculating a Selling Price

Once a business has decided on the broad pricing strategy for its product or service it then has to calculate an actual selling price. This can be done in a variety of ways. Two common methods are shown below.

Cost-plus pricing

A manufacturer or retailer will calculate the cost of making or buying a product and add a set percentage profit to arrive at their selling price.

Cost of manufacturing a tin of baked beans	£0.30
30% mark-up	£0.09
Selling price	£0.39

Different businesses will use different rates of mark-up. A supermarket adds different mark-ups to different products. It may add 30% on to a tin of beans. In contrast a car dealership may only add between 2 and 5% on a new car and approximately 10% on a used car.

Cost-plus pricing is often used by small businesses as it is a very simple method of setting a selling price. It is also used by some large volume businesses such as supermarkets.

Contribution pricing

A business using this method will calculate the direct costs of making or buying a product, namely staff wages and raw materials. A contribution toward the fixed costs of the business, e.g. salaries, rent and loan repayments are then added. Any amount after covering fixed costs is profit for the business.

For example, a business producing conservatories may have fixed costs of £100 000 per year, representing the sales staff's salaries, rent and business rates. The business may expect to sell 100 conservatories per year. Each one sold therefore has to generate £1000 towards covering the fixed costs. On average £1000 needs to be added to the cost of buying in each conservatory to break even. If £1500 is added to the direct cost of each conservatory it will generate £500 profit for the business.

Channel of distribution	the route that products take to reach the customer from the manufacturer.

How a product goes from manufacturer to customer is called the channel of distribution. The following routes are possible:

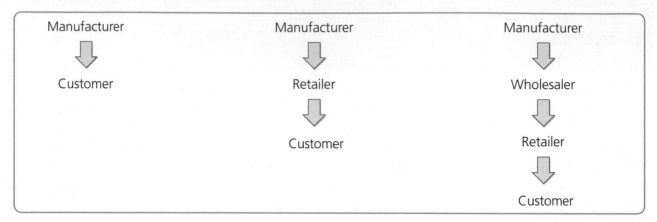

The channel of distribution chosen depends on a variety of factors, including:

- **The product being sold.** If the product is highly technical and expert knowledge is required to sell it, then selling is often done directly from the manufacturer (e.g. mechanical equipment being sold to a hospital). In contrast, mass market foodstuffs are usually distributed through a wholesaler and retailer before reaching the customer.

- **The finance available to the organisation.**

- **The reliability of companies in the chain.** If a wholesaler or retailer is unreliable in their part of the distribution process, a manufacturer may decide to supply directly to the customer.

- **The desired image for the product.** When Häagen-Dazs was first launched, it was only available in exclusive outlets. When it had attained an upmarket image, it was made more widely available through supermarkets.

- **Government restrictions.** For example, certain medicines can only be sold via prescription in pharmacies.

- **The product's life-cycle.** If a product is in its introductory phase, it is perhaps sold only through more exclusive retail outlets where a premium price can be charged.

- **The manufacturer's distribution capability.** If the manufacturer does not possess a delivery fleet or a sales force then it may distribute through a wholesaler.

Direct Selling

Method	Description
Internet selling	Many organisations now sell their products and services via the internet, taking payment by credit or debit card. This allows a business to reach a global market. Customer information is also easily collected to target offers and promotions effectively. It is attractive to customers as they can order online from home, saving time and hassle in shopping. However, many customers fear using the internet to purchase products as some sites are insecure regarding credit card details. Some products are also often more expensive to purchase over the internet than in the high street due to the extra cost of postage and packaging.
Mail order 	These are goods sold to customers through catalogues (e.g. Next and Kays). There is a large growth in mail order due to the convenience of shopping from home, often with credit facilities available. Mail order only companies save costs as few sales staff may be required and they tend not to require expensive high street locations. Some mail order products are exclusive (i.e. only available through mail order). Some companies who sell by mail order also sell from their own website. Some customers dislike mail order shopping due to the lack of personal contact with the retailer and the high delivery charges. Companies may incur high advertising and administration costs. A high level of bad debt is possible.
Direct mail 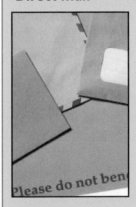	This involves a company posting promotional letters, brochures or leaflets about its products or services to homes and workplaces. These can then be ordered by post or over the telephone. *Reader's Digest* is an example of a company which uses direct mail. Customers within certain market segments can be targeted. A company can also reach customers in a wide geographical area. Personalised letters generated through mail merges can improve direct mail sales. However, some customers do not like the vast amount of direct mail they receive – they call this 'junk' mail. Also, mailing lists of potential customers can very quickly become out of date so mail can go to the wrong people, costing the company extra money and possibly upsetting these people.
Newspaper/ magazine selling	Companies place adverts in newspapers/magazines describing and showing their product for sale. Customers respond directly to adverts by filling in coupons to post, or by telephone.
Personal selling	Some companies employ sales staff who sell products door-to-door or by telephone (called 'tele-sales'). For example, pharmaceutical companies employ sales representatives (reps) to visit doctors' surgeries to encourage doctors to prescribe certain medicines. Double-glazing and kitchens are also often sold by personal selling. Personal selling allows the product to be demonstrated, benefits and technical details to be explained and feedback to be received from potential customers.

There are different types of retailer. Manufacturers must decide which type of retailer to sell their products through. Manufacturers sell products to a retailer because:

- they are often located close to customers
- retailers may offer credit facilities, delivery, after-sales service and guarantees
- retailers may already have an established customer base
- retailers incur costs of storage of stocks, retail premises and sales staff
- selling to a retailer is more direct than through a wholesaler. The more direct the channel of distribution, the higher the percentage profit for the manufacturer.

Retailer	Description
Independent store	An independent retailer tends to be a small business, with one or only a few stores. It will often purchase its products through a wholesaler. The prices in an independent store will often be higher than in bigger chains as independents might not be able to buy directly from manufacturers and take advantage of bulk buying discounts. They tend to stock branded goods. Corner shops, small clothes boutiques and gift shops tend to be independent stores.
Supermarket	A supermarket is a large self-service store selling food and household products. Supermarkets often purchase directly from manufacturers and can also receive bulk buying discounts. Supermarkets often stock thousands of different products at any one time, including food, clothing and music items. Supermarkets sell branded goods as well as their own label ranges. Morrisons, Tesco and ASDA are all examples of supermarkets.
Chain store	A chain store company has many stores with the same name in different geographical locations. They specialise in a particular type of product. HMV, Next, JJB Sports and WH Smith are all examples of chain stores. They are usually located in busy high streets or in shopping centres.
Department store	Department stores tend to stock branded goods. They tend to have a variety of departments specialising in, for example, ladies' clothing, men's clothing and household products. They tend to be situated in prime city/town centre locations, and have an upmarket image. Debenhams, John Lewis and Frasers are all examples of department stores.
Discount store	Matalan, Primark and TK Maxx are all examples of discount stores. They tend to sell large quantities of a limited range of products at discount prices. Displays are kept to a minimum to minimise costs. Discount stores are usually not located in prime high street sites.

Retailing trends

- Increase in out-of-town shopping centres. Most large towns now have retail parks or shopping centres on their outskirts. Many people prefer the convenience of having all shops under one roof. These centres usually also have food outlets, leisure facilities for children and easy parking.
- Extended opening hours to fit in with people's work and leisure times. For example, some supermarkets are now open 24 hours a day.
- Increased domination of the supermarkets. Large supermarkets now sell petrol, pharmacy products, clothing, music and electrical goods in addition to their traditional foodstuffs. With Wal-Mart having taken over ASDA, the trend of supermarkets selling a wider variety of products is set to continue.
- Increase in internet shopping.

Wholesalers

A wholesaler purchases goods in bulk, directly from a manufacturer and then sells in smaller quantities to retailers and other businesses. Examples of wholesalers include Booker, Makro and Costco.

Manufacturers sell products to a wholesaler because:

- it saves the manufacturer from making many small deliveries to individual retailers, therefore saving on transport, administration and sales rep costs
- it saves the manufacturer from high stockholding costs (as the wholesaler purchases in bulk)
- it saves the manufacturer from being left with stock if customer tastes or fashions change
- it can save the manufacturer from labelling its product for retailers, as the wholesaler will sometimes do this for them.

However, not all manufacturers decide to use wholesalers. Some manufacturers decide to keep complete control over the way their product is presented to retailers and customers.

Promotion

| *Promotion* | the way in which a customer is made aware of a product or service and is persuaded to purchase it. |

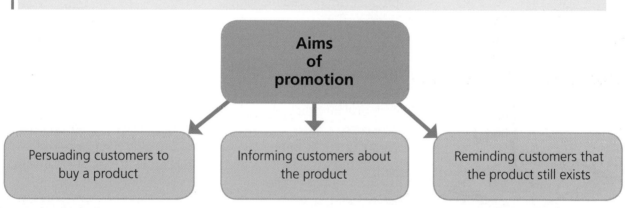

Promotion includes:

- advertising
- into and out of the pipeline sales promotions
- public relations.

Advertising

Informative adverts are used to increase awareness of a product or service and to inform the consumer about the product or service being offered. For example, adverts in the *Yellow Pages* tend to be informative by listing services offered.

Persuasive adverts aim to persuade a customer to buy a product by stressing that it is very desirable to have. Most adverts have a degree of persuasion.

Product endorsement occurs when famous sports or showbiz personalities are paid to wear and use a particular product. For example, Adidas pay David Beckham and Nike pay Tiger Woods to wear their products.

Product placement involves a firm paying for its products to be used in films or TV programmes. For example, BMW paid for James Bond to be seen driving its cars in *Goldeneye*, *Tomorrow Never Dies* and *The World is Not Enough*.

CASE STUDY

Product placement in films is now commonplace. In the 2004 film *I Robot*, **JVC**, **Converse**, **Fed Ex** and **Audi** were all featured.

Other types of product placement are now becoming more common. **Hewlett Packard** place their products in room layout pictures for **IKEA** catalogues.

Product placement is also now used in video games.

Adapted from www.brandhype.org

Advertising media	✔ Advantages ✔	✘ Disadvantages ✘
Television 	■ Adverts can be targeted to a large national audience covering all market segments. ■ The products can be made appealing by using colour, sound and movement in the advert. ■ The product can be demonstrated. ■ With regular adverts the product can maintain a high profile.	■ Television advertising is expensive. ■ The product may not need to reach all market segments. ■ The message can be short-lived. ■ Many viewers channel surf when the adverts come on.
National daily newspapers 	■ National exposure can be gained. ■ Technical information can be explained. ■ Products can be aimed at certain market segments by careful choice of paper to advertise in. ■ Readers can cut out and keep adverts for future reference.	■ People tend not to scrutinise daily newspapers. ■ No sound or movement can be shown and adverts are often in black and white. ■ Can be expensive to ensure a wide national coverage.
Sunday newspapers 	■ People tend to have the time to scrutinise their Sunday paper. ■ Large national circulation. ■ Sunday supplements are printed in colour, allowing adverts to have more impact.	■ Can be expensive to place an advert.
Local newspapers 	■ Good for targeting local audiences. ■ Local readers tend to scrutinise the paper.	■ Often a poorer quality production than national newspapers.

Advertising media	✔ Advantages ✔	✘ Disadvantages ✘
Magazines 	■ Colour adverts have a bigger impact. ■ Can target a particular market segment by advertising in special interest magazines. ■ Magazines are often kept for future reference.	■ Can be expensive to place an advert.
Independent radio 	■ Cheaper to advertise than on television. ■ Can have a captive audience as listeners tend not to channel surf when adverts come on. ■ Can target particular market segments by advertising on particular radio stations or during particular shows.	■ Listeners often do not pay attention to the adverts. ■ Limited to sound only. ■ Reliant on the listeners' imagination for the advert to be successful.
Cinema 	■ There is a captive audience. ■ Adverts can be shown before particular films to appeal to particular market segments.	■ The message tends to be short-lived. ■ Limited audience.
Outdoor media 	■ Can attract a wide target audience. ■ Often in busy locations – therefore can have a high visual impact. ■ Passers-by will frequently see the advert.	■ Can suffer weather deterioration or be subject to vandalism. ■ Passers-by may view it as part of the scenery and ignore it. ■ Can be expensive to advertise (e.g. on football hoardings).
Internet 	■ Can be relatively cheap ■ Adverts can target particular market segments if placed on the correct website. ■ Adverts can be changed easily.	■ Web surfers may ignore adverts.
Direct mail 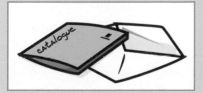	■ Can target particular market segments.	■ Customers tend to dislike junk mail. ■ Need to target mail accurately to intended customers otherwise little interest will be generated in the product.

The choice of advertising media depends on:

- the product to be advertised
- the market segment to be targeted
- the type of coverage required (national or local)
- the advertising budget available
- how competitors advertise their products
- how technical the product is
- the size of the organisation
- legal restrictions (e.g. tobacco products cannot be advertised on TV).

Controls on advertising

The Advertising Standards Authority (ASA) is an organisation that monitors all advertising, sales, promotions and direct marketing. It covers newspapers, magazines, billboards, text messages, internet banner adverts, radio and TV. If an advert is found to be offensive or untruthful, the ASA can ask the advertiser to withdraw or amend the advert.

The Trades Description Act 1968 states that a product must be advertised in an honest way which is not misleading to consumers.

CASE STUDY

ADVERTISING MEDIA BY PERCENTAGE – 2004

Press	47.50%
TV	25.80%
Direct Mail	13.40%
Outdoor	5.40%
Internet	3.60%
Radio	3.30%
Cinema	1%

Adapted from www.adassorc.org.uk

Sales Promotions

Sales promotions   short-term inducements used to encourage sales.

There are two groups of sales promotion:

Into the pipeline promotions

These are offered by manufacturers to retailers (dealers) to encourage them to stock their products:

- point of sale displays
- dealer loaders
- sale or return
- dealer competitions/bonuses
- staff training
- credit facilities.

Out of the pipeline promotions

These are offered by the retailer to the final customer to encourage purchases to be made:

- free samples
- credit facilities
- demonstrations
- competitions
- Buy One Get One Frees (BOGOFs)
- bonus packs
- free offers
- coupons/vouchers.

Into the pipeline promotions	Out of the pipeline promotions
Point of sale materials such as posters, racks to hold videos or leaflets, window display materials or in-store displays are often provided free of charge. For example, Disneyland Paris provides UK travel agents with boards and posters to use as window displays advertising Disneyland Paris.	**Free samples** are often used to encourage purchase. For example, perfume companies often produce perfume samples to be handed out by retailers at perfume counters.
Dealer loaders are used as inducements to attract orders (e.g. 'buy ten get one free').	**Credit facilities** are often given to customers to allow them to obtain a product that they otherwise could not afford, by paying for it at a later date.
Sale or return can be used to encourage a retailer to stock an untried product as it may remove the fear of being left with unsold stock.	**Demonstrations** at the point of sale involve giving samples to encourage a sale. For example, car dealers offer test drives.
Dealer competitions can be linked to dealer sales with attractive prizes for the most successful dealer. Car manufacturers may offer holidays as prizes for dealers who meet sales targets.	**Competitions** in which customers have to buy the product to allow them to enter are offered on the product's packaging, and in magazines and newspapers. Newspapers make great use of these to encourage purchasers to buy their paper by using, for example, 'Lucky Wallets', free holidays and scratchcards.
Staff training is often provided by the manufacturer if its product requires technical explanations or demonstrations. For example, car manufacturers offer dealers staff training which covers technical issues with new cars, how to promote the cars and customer service.	**Buy One Get One Free (BOGOF)** is often used by supermarkets on selected products for a limited time.
Credit facilities often encourage retailers to stock a product. The retailer pays for the goods at a later date agreed with the manufacturer.	**Bonus packs** offer more of the product for the same price as the original (e.g. 15% extra free).
	Free offers are often used by magazines where a free CD/DVD is given with the purchase of the magazine or a free toy in a box of breakfast cereal.
	Coupons and vouchers can be printed in newspapers, on the reverse of till receipts and in customer magazines. They allow customers money off future purchases.

CASE STUDY

In 1992 **Hoover** decided to launch a promotion to shift a backlog of vacuum cleaners and washing machines sitting in their warehouse. It ended up costing **Hoover** £48 million and much more in bad publicity.

The promotion was simple. Spend £100 on any **Hoover** product and get two free return flights initially to Europe and later to the USA. **Hoover** expected approximately 5000 flights to be taken.

The company were inundated and could not meet demand, there were not enough plane seats and a lengthy 6 year legal battle between customers and **Hoover** occurred. Eventually more than 200 000 took up the offer and did actually fly.

Three senior executives lost their jobs and at its peak 250 **Hoover** staff were managing the problem. It is regarded as one of the biggest marketing fiascos the UK has seen.

Adapted from www.bbc.co.uk

Public Relations

Public Relations (PR) are the activities of an organisation which help it improve its image locally, nationally and internationally. PR includes organising donations to charities, event sponsorship, product endorsement, publicity literature, merchandising (e.g. providing corporate calendars and gifts), press conferences and press releases.

PR staff have the task of responding to bad publicity. To counteract bad publicity, a PR Manager often makes a press release to the media, either denying problems or accepting responsibility and so aims to create positive publicity to counteract the bad.

Quick Questions

1   Identify the factors that influence the price a product is set at.
2   Explain four different pricing strategies.
3   Identify the factors that can affect the choice of channel of distribution.
4   Explain three different direct selling techniques.
5   Why does a manufacturer use a retailer as a distribution channel?
6   Name four different advertising media and give a cost and benefit of each.
7   What controls exist to monitor advertising?
8   Define the terms price, product, place and promotion.
9   Give a definition of into and out of the pipeline promotions.
10 What type of activities does a PR executive organise?

Extended Response Questions

INTERMEDIATE 2

1 *Distinguish* between field and desk research. (5 marks)

2 *Identify* and *describe* three field research techniques. *Give* one advantage and one disadvantage of each. (12 marks)

3 *Describe* the stages of the product life cycle. Use a diagram to support your answer. (8 marks)

4 *Define* the term 'brand'. *Give* an advantage and a disadvantage of a brand for a customer. (3 marks)

5 *Identify* and *describe* three pricing strategies. *Give* an example of when it would be appropriate to use each. (9 marks)

6 *Describe* the factors that influence the channel of distribution a manufacturer chooses for its product. (4 marks)

7 *Outline* the main features of direct mail. (3 marks)

8 Newspaper, magazine and TV advertising are the most common methods to use for advertising. *Identify* three other methods of advertising. *Give* an advantage and a disadvantage of each. (9 marks)

> **Hint**
> Remember to label your diagrams.

HIGHER

1 *Describe* the following marketing terms:
- Product orientation
- Industrial market
- Differentiated marketing. (3 marks)

2 Formé is a retailer that sells quality maternity clothing to pregnant women. This is an example of niche marketing. *Describe* what is meant by 'niche marketing'. *Outline* why niche marketing is attractive and the risks that may be faced. (5 marks)

3 *Explain* why businesses spend large amounts of finance on market research. (6 marks)

4 Some organisations use stratified random sampling when selecting who to gather information from. *Describe* two other sampling methods that an organisation could use. *Justify* your choices. (4 marks)

5 The confectionary market is a very competitive one. Manufacturers seek ways to prolong the life of each confectionary brand. *Describe* the ways in which a confectionary manufacturer can prolong the life of its product. *Use* a diagram to support your answer. (6 marks)

6 *Explain* the pricing strategies that a new business might employ when introducing a new product onto the market. (8 marks)

7 In the introduction phase of its product life cycle Radley handbags were only available in large, well-known department stores. They are now much more widely available in many gift and accessory shops. *Describe* other factors that could influence a business' decision on where to sell its products. (5 marks)

8 Marks & Spencer launched a high profile TV, press, radio and billboard advertising campaign in 2005 featuring their range of ladies clothing and foodstuffs. *Describe* three other methods of advertising that they could have used. *Justify* your choices. (6 marks)

9 *Describe* the promotional strategies that a biscuit manufacturer such as McVities might employ when introducing a new product onto the market. (4 marks)

> **Operations** is vital to any organisation as making products and producing services to sell is vital to an organisation's objectives of making a profit and generating wealth.

Role and Importance of Operations

Higher

The operations function in an organisation is one of the core activities of any business. It produces the products and services that are sold to generate a profit. It is not only manufacturers that have an operations function. Arnold Clark has an Operations Manager as do Stagecoach for each of their 20 regional UK companies. They are responsible for the day-to-day management of the service provided and for ensuring that services are delivered to customers smoothly and efficiently.

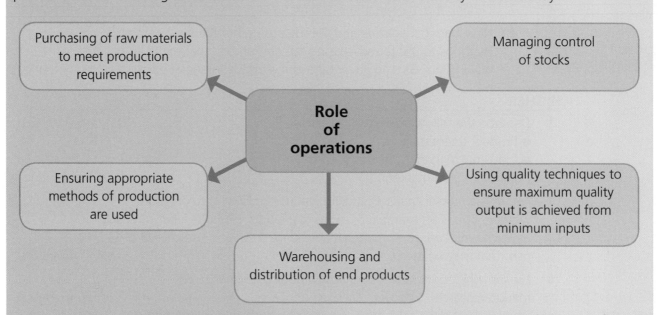

Operations can be split into three key elements where Operations Managers have to make fundamental decisions.

Purchasing

It has to be decided what stock to purchase, how much and who from. The elements that make this up are covered in the Purchase of Materials on page 77.

System design

Operations managers have to decide on a layout of the factory and production processes that will ensure efficient flow of work between different production areas. They also have to plan what staff are required and for what purpose, whether production will be labour or capital intensive and the degree of automation (machinery and robots) that will be used.

System operation

Decisions have to be made regarding how best to control the flow of stocks to ensure the production process or final customer's requirements are met. They must also make decisions such as ensuring that there is sufficient storage room available for stocks and that facilities are appropriate for the stock to minimise deterioration or theft.

Input, Process, Output

There are three stages in successful operating systems:

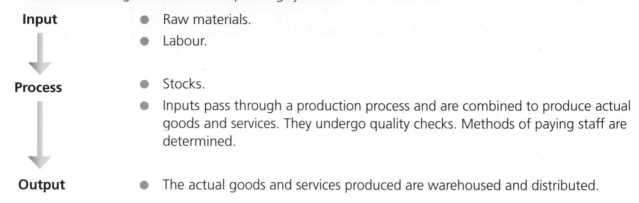

Input
- Raw materials.
- Labour.

Process
- Stocks.
- Inputs pass through a production process and are combined to produce actual goods and services. They undergo quality checks. Methods of paying staff are determined.

Output
- The actual goods and services produced are warehoused and distributed.

Purchase of Materials

Decisions have to be made as to how much raw material (the quantity) and from whom raw materials are to be purchased (the supplier).

The quantity of raw materials ordered depends on four main issues:

- stock of raw materials currently available
- duration of time which will elapse between this order and any future orders
- amount of raw materials likely to be required during this period
- storage space available and cost of storage.

Other factors to be considered include: normal spoilage during production; provision of some buffer stock; minimisation of stockholding whilst maintaining adequate supplies; available finance.

Once these issues have been considered, it has to be decided which supplier offers the best terms. The following factors should be taken into account:

- **Quality** – A supplier's quality should be acceptable and consistent for the firm's needs.
- **Quantity** – A supplier should be able to deliver the correct quantity.
- **Time** – A supplier should be able to meet the firm's delivery date requirements.
- **Dependability** – The source of supply should be dependable, the supplier must be respectable and likely to stay in business, and have reliable delivery systems.
- **Price** – The lowest price for the quality desired should be sought to ensure value for money; discounts available for regular customers/bulk orders should be checked; availability of credit terms.
- **Location** of supplier – Additional charges for delivery or insurance should be checked.

Firms must use the correct mix of the above when deciding on a supplier and quantity. This is known as the **purchasing mix**.

Stocks	Raw materials, work in progress and finished goods.

Having stocks enables goods to be available for immediate use in production or for delivery to customers; shows the range of goods available for production; enables customer demand to be met; allows bulk buying to take place to gain discounts.

Having too much stock can result in high storage costs; high maintenance costs; high security costs; high insurance costs; lighting and handling costs; a large amount of space being taken up; money tied up when it could be used elsewhere more profitably; stocks left unsold that may deteriorate, become obsolete or become spoiled; theft by employees.

Having too little stock can result in a business being unable to cope with unexpected changes in demand if its stocks are too low; if future deliveries are delayed the firm may run out of stock and therefore have to stop production; the firm is less able to cope with unexpected shortages of materials; firms holding low stocks may have to place more orders, therefore raising ordering/administration costs; out-of-stock costs (costs of lost revenue and profit due to lost sales as customers cannot be supplied from stock). A business may gain a poor reputation if it cannot supply customers resulting in them losing customers to a competitor.

Effective stock control involves the following:

Set a maximum stock level (economic level)

This is the level of appropriate stock which should be held for the organisation to minimise costs. When setting this level a business should take into account storage space available, stock security measures, cost of storage facilities and finance available to purchase and be tied up in stock.

Set a minimum stock level

A minimum stock level is the level that stock must not fall below as shortages in raw materials may result in reduced output. When setting this level a business should take into account ordering and delivery times.

Set a re-order level

This is the point at which new stocks should be ordered. As items are taken from stock, the amount left for use reduces and at some point new stock has to be ordered. This is calculated by considering average daily usage and the time taken to receive new supplies (i.e. the **lead time**).

A pattern of effective stock control is shown in the following diagram below.

Set a re-order quantity

Once the re-order level is reached, a standard quantity is automatically requested. On receipt of the delivery, the maximum stock level should be achieved.

Hint

Include a relevant diagram in stock usage questions. Remember to label your diagram.

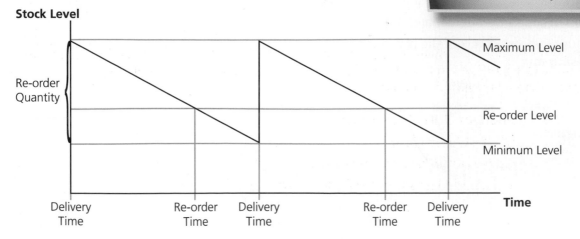

Control of stock

It is often someone's responsibility to monitor, control and record stock to avoid theft, waste or shortage occurring. A general procedure which should be followed to allow stock to be monitored, controlled and recorded is:

- materials should only be issued to departments after receiving a stock requisition from them (a form requesting materials which has an authorised signature)
- stock levels should be recorded on stock record cards or held on a computer database. These record stock used or issued to departments, and received from suppliers. Totals should match the actual levels on shelves.

Computerised stock control

Many organisations hold their stock details on a computer database. This helps to keep balances up-to-date after stock has been received and issued. Some are programmed to order more stock automatically as the re-order level is reached. Supermarkets use bar codes to help in stock control – as each item is scanned at the checkout one is taken from the recorded stock level. This allows the manager to check stock levels, total stock values and the store's sales easily at any time of the day. Best sellers and slow-moving lines can also be easily identified. Computerised stock control can be costly to set up and operate due to hardware, software and update costs.

Storage of stock

Supplies of stocks can be held in one central storage area (centralised) or be located in the different areas in which they are used (decentralised).

Advantages of centralised stock storage

- Improved security from loss or theft as it tends to be carefully controlled by specialist staff.
- Specialist staff maintain stocks by following agreed procedures for its control – only issued when 'authorised'.
- Central stock of components or materials may cost less to hold than many small 'on-site' supplies.
- Improved efficiency in stock handling and management.

Advantages of decentralised stock storage

- Stock is always 'at hand' when required.
- Orders of new stock reflect actual production usage or sales levels.
- Speedier turnover of a small quantity of stock reduces the likelihood of its deterioration or decay.

Just in Time (JIT)

H *Higher*

Just in Time (JIT) Production is a Japanese approach to production that involves keeping the stock levels (therefore costs) to a minimum. Stocks arrive just in time to be used in production. Goods are not produced unless the firm has an order from a customer.

Successful JIT depends on:

- reliable suppliers
- good quality control procedures
- access to a supply of skilled workers.

✔ Advantages ✔	✘ Disadvantages ✘
■ Valuable capital is not tied up in stocks and can therefore be used elsewhere more profitably. ■ Less space required for stock therefore reduced warehousing costs. ■ Closer relationships with suppliers. ■ Reduced deterioration, or waste of stock. ■ Less vulnerability to fashion and technology changes. ■ Reduction in stockholding costs. ■ Increase in cash flow.	■ Danger of disrupted production due to non-arrival of supplies. ■ Danger of lost sales. ■ High dependence on suppliers. ■ Less time for quality control on arrival of materials. ■ Increased ordering and administration costs. ■ May lose bulk-buying discounts. ■ Increase in suppliers' transport costs. ■ Increased chance of transport failures. ■ Increased volume of traffic on road (many small loads instead of fewer large loads).

CASE STUDY

Limerick in Ireland is home to **Dell**'s European computer manufacturing operation. **Dell** uses the JIT system of stock control. It does not have stocks of components, therefore, can sell to the customer at a lower price.

They only manufacture a computer when an order is placed. If new technology emerges products can be altered immediately. If it had stocks of completed computers it could not do this.

Raw materials are delivered just in time through 40 dock doors on one side of the building, manufactured by teams and rigorously tested. The finished computers are then dispatched via another 40 doors on the other side of the building, destined for direct delivery to customers' offices and homes throughout Europe, Middle East and Africa.

Adapted from www.dell.co.uk

Kanban

Higher

This is another Japanese system. It uses markers, such as flags or lights, to order movement of stocks between different stages of production. If a flag is up on a stock item then it indicates that the item should be reordered. This is useful if JIT is to function properly to prevent a build up of stocks or parts in a factory.

Markers are used to tell the stockroom to take a part to a particular production line destination. If a production worker requires restocking of a part, he/she puts his/her flag up or light on. Markers can also be used to tell employees to begin production, to add their output to stock or to tell external suppliers to send stock to a particular factory destination.

A business can pay its employees by various methods.

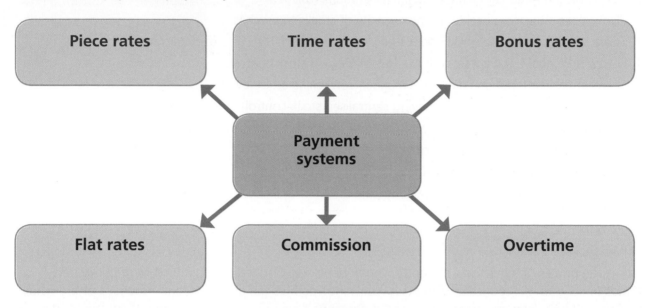

System	Description
Flat rate	Some employees are paid a set salary per annum. This salary is then divided into twelve equal monthly payments. Managers, supervisors and office staff tend to be paid by this method. It does not reward staff for an increased high level of effort but allows them a guaranteed monthly income.
Piece rate	This involves workers being paid per item they produce. There is also a low basic flat rate with additional earnings made through piece rate. This method of payment tends to be used in factories. The more a worker produces, the higher the rate of pay. It can act as an incentive to employees to work hard. Close supervision of output is required to ensure that workers do not sacrifice quality for quantity. Employees may be penalised if quality is not maintained.
Time rate	Many workers are paid per hour worked (e.g. £6.50 per hour). Staff in service sector organisations and manual workers are often paid at time rates. This method is simple to calculate for the employer and rewards the employee for the time spent at work. It does not provide any added incentive to produce quality work.
Overtime	When employees work a set number of hours, overtime may be offered for them to work extra hours. Their normal hourly time rate usually rises for any overtime worked (e.g. 'double-time').
Bonus rate	Some workers are paid a basic wage with additional payments (bonuses) received when they meet agreed productivity, time-keeping and/or efficiency targets. The bonus is added onto their basic wage.
Commission	In many organisations (e.g. in some car showrooms and double-glazing companies) sales commission may be the sole method of paying employees or it might be added onto a basic wage/salary. Commission is usually calculated as a percentage of the products' sales value. It is used as an incentive by employers for employees to sell more. Supervisors, however, must check the sales technique used by sales staff to ensure that they are not using rogue selling techniques.

Production

This is the process in which raw materials, components and finished goods are converted into new goods or services. A production plan is set which incorporates the objectives and functions of the whole business. Before production can begin, major decisions have to be taken regarding: plant layout; degree of automation; scale of production; method of production; and type of quality controls required.

Methods of Production

Method of production

Job production

Job production is where a single product is custom-made to a customer's own specification. Bridges, wedding cakes and oil rig platforms are made using job production.

✔ Advantages ✔	✘ Disadvantages ✘
■ Firms can produce one-off orders exactly to meet customer demand. ■ A high price may be charged. ■ Specifications can be changed by customers even if production has started. ■ Workers are more likely to be motivated as there is a variety of work and skills required.	■ Expensive due to high skill of staff needed – therefore high wages. ■ High research and development, administration and transport costs. ■ A wide variety of equipment/tools is required. ■ Lead times can be lengthy.

CASE STUDY

The **Cake and Chocolate Shop** is a specialist cake producer based in Edinburgh. It only produces one-off custom designed cakes for weddings, anniversaries, birthdays and corporate events. Prices range from £30–£80 for a birthday cake.

The production method is labour-intensive as making and decorating the cakes requires considerable skill and time. This can ensure that quality is maintained at all stages of production. A high price is charged compared to mass produced bakery and supermarket cakes which accounts for the time, skill and unique nature of each cake.

Method of Production

Batch production

Batch production is the production of groups of similar products. No item in a group goes to the next stage until all are ready. For example, newspapers, bread and houses in a new estate are often produced in batches.

✔ Advantages ✔	✘ Disadvantages ✘
■ Batches can be changed to meet specific customer requirements. ■ Reduced need for costly, highly skilled staff. ■ Machinery can be relatively standardised, which reduces costs.	■ Machines/workers may sit idle between stages and between each batch unless there is careful planning. ■ Expensive machinery may be required due to staff being less skilled. ■ Stock levels may be high. ■ Staff may be less motivated as they repeat the same tasks in batches. ■ If batches are small, costs will still be high.

CASE STUDY

Anne Dorward is a sole trader who runs **Dunlop Dairy** in Ayrshire. She milks sheep, goats and cattle to provide the raw materials for the nine different cheeses her business makes.

Monday, Wednesday and Friday are cheese making days. Two batches of cheese are produced on each day. Aiket, a soft cheese, is produced from a tank of milk that is worked for a day. When ready, the cheese is poured into moulds that are then drained. When the entire group of moulds has been drained they are then stored for a month to ripen. After a month the batch of cheese is packaged ready for sale in 200 g units.

If a wholesaler requested 400 g cheeses for a particular customer a batch of these could be accommodated.

Method of production

Flow production

Flow production is a process in which production items move continuously from one operation to the next. Each part of the process leads to the eventual production of the final product with the aid of machinery to save labour costs. Products are produced to a standard specification. Cars, bottled products and some electrical products (e.g. TVs) are examples of products which are often produced using flow production methods.

✔ Advantages ✔	✘ Disadvantages ✘
■ Costs are spread over a large number of goods. Therefore the cost per item is reduced (economies of scale are achieved). ■ Bulk discounts are likely to be gained in purchasing raw materials. ■ Huge quantities can be produced. ■ The process is often automated, which lowers labour costs and human error. ■ Machinery can work 24/7.	■ Huge investment to set up is needed. ■ Individual customer requirements cannot be met. ■ Equipment may be inflexible and may not be suitable for more than one purpose. ■ Worker motivation can be low because of the repetitive nature of the job. ■ Breakdowns can be very costly.

CASE STUDY

Highland Spring manufactures a range of still and sparkling natural mineral water products.

The Perthshire based company boasts one of the most modern flow production bottling plants in Europe from where they export to over 50 different countries. The factory produces over 69 000 bottles per hour on four production lines that operate 24 hours a day, seven days a week. Production lines are fully automated with little staff input other than staff involved in controlling the production line, loading and unloading bottles, cleaning, quality control checks and maintenance.

There are plans in 2006 to spend £15 million to expand production to five production lines.

The choice of production method depends on:

- the product being produced
- the size of the market
- the size of the business
- the finance available
- the technology available.

Labour-Intensive v Capital-Intensive Production

Most manufacturing companies use a mix of labour-intensive and capital-intensive (machine-intensive) production. The actual mix used determines the degree of automation. The greater the reliance on machines, the greater the automation.

Labour-intensive production

Some manufacturers rely heavily on their workforce rather than machinery to manufacture their products. This occurs when:

- labour supply is cheap and readily available
- the product requires craftsmanship or special expertise to produce.
- the business is small and does not have the finance to purchase expensive machinery.

Being labour-intensive is not without its costs:

- A skilled labour force can be expensive to pay and train.
- It may be limited to small scale production – cannot take advantage of economies of scale.
- If staff are ill or absent then production may halt.
- The quality of products has to be monitored closely to ensure consistency.

Capital-intensive production

Other manufacturers rely heavily on machinery and automation in their production process. This occurs when:

- a standard product is being produced with standard operations
- labour supply is scarce or expensive
- consistency of product and quality is required
- economies of scale is desirable
- continuous production is required.

Being capital-intensive has a number of costs:

- Set-up costs of machinery can be very high.
- Lost production time during breakdowns is very costly.
- Individual customer requirements cannot be met.
- Worker motivation can be low due to repetitive nature of tasks.

Efficiency of Production

In order to monitor and control production, the efficiency of the production process and manufacturing workers' practices must be scrutinised.

To identify the most efficient use of production resources, a work study can be carried out. This is an analysis of the working methods, equipment and materials that are used in order to identify the most efficient way of doing a task or job. It is then possible to set standards of practice, to choose materials and to decide on machines and use of time. Work studies are carried out in two main ways:

Method study

This provides information on how tasks are done at present with a view to improving practices for the future. The acronym **SREDIM** describes what a method study does:

Select the task to be analysed

Record how it is currently done

Examine the information collected

Develop a better method of doing the task

Install the new method

Maintain the new method

For example, in a garage, a method study involves developing improved procedures for servicing cars.

Work measurement

This establishes how long tasks should take so that standard times can be identified for each task. Actual employee performance can then be judged against the standard task times.

For example, in a garage, work measurement involves setting a standard time to be spent servicing each car.

Quality

Organisations in the UK use a variety of measures to ensure that their products/services meet a high level of quality. These include: **benchmarking**, **quality control, quality assurance, quality circles**, **quality management** and **British Standards**.

CASE STUDY

Thomas Tunnock Limited of Uddingston use flow production to produce a range of biscuit products including Caramel Wafers, Caramel Logs, Teacakes and Snowballs.

Raw material ingredients delivered to the factory are accompanied with a certificate of analysis or conformance. They are inspected and random samples are taken and sent for chemical and microbiological analysis. Packaging materials are checked to ensure colours are correct.

The factory makes its own caramel and chocolate for use in biscuit production. These undergo weight control, texture and visual quality checks.

Hourly quality checks and product assessments are made during production by selecting a packet from each production line to check for condition of packaging, correct date code, etc. Each biscuit in a packet is then checked for alignment of wrapper and that the biscuit is complete and undamaged. In addition, daily product samples are taken and retained for a maximum of two years.

Tunnocks are accredited to ISO9001 for Quality Management Systems and a British Retail Consortium Technical Standard for Food Safety.

A customer may view a quality product as one that uses a high quality of materials, has a high standard of workmanship, works perfectly, is reliable and is to the specification stated on the packaging or other product literature.

If a business develops and manufactures a quality product, it may find it easier to satisfy customer demands, meet safety standards and legal requirements, and ensure the product works properly or can be repaired easily. The company may be able to charge a premium price and have a high status in the market.

Benchmarking

Identifying a benchmark is used as a method of improving quality of production or service by copying the best techniques used by another organisation regarded as the 'best'. A company which is the first to use benchmarking in its market will hope to be regarded as the benchmark standard in the future. Setting a benchmark as a target can be very motivating for staff and can create a culture where continual improvement is standard practice.

Quality control

A manufacturer passes a sample of their raw materials and the final product through a quality control check. Any unacceptable products are then discarded as waste or sent back for reworking. This ensures that substandard products are not sold to customers.

Quality assurance

At certain points in the production process, products are checked to ensure that they meet agreed quality standards. All aspects of the production process are looked at to ensure errors do not occur.

Quality circles

These involve small groups of workers meeting at regular intervals to discuss where improvements can be made in the production process. Suggestions are then made to management for approval before being implemented. By including them in quality circles, workers should be more motivated, more productive and more willing to introduce new production methods.

Higher

Quality management

This is a system of doing things right the first time. No errors are tolerated. All staff, regardless of their position in the organisation, are involved in ensuring absolute quality of their work. Work processes are scrutinised. Teams/quality circles constantly strive to make processes more efficient and reduce waste.

Commitment to quality management requires a clearly defined quality policy; focus on customer satisfaction; substantial staff training; constant auditing to ensure the process is working; teamwork at all levels; employee empowerment and a commitment from all staff regardless of their position in the organisation.

British Standards Institution

The British Standards Institution (BSI) is an organisation that produces national standards for certain products. When a business produces a product and proves it meets the agreed quality and safety standards specified by the BSI, the product will be marked with a BS 'Kitemark' symbol. This may be able to give an organisation a competitive advantage, however, the process and paperwork involved in gaining a BSI standard may be lengthy. This gives consumers confidence in the product because it has reached agreed BSI standards. There are also many international standards (IS numbers) an organisation can gain.

For example, at petrol stations the BS standard BS EN 228 is displayed on pumps where unleaded fuel meets agreed quality standards.

Other trade organisations

Certain trade organisations introduce standards and logos that can be displayed on products that have met agreed quality standards that they have specified. There are quality assurance stickers that are displayed on meat products that have been produced to a certain industry standard. For example, eggs carry a Red Lion Quality mark to identify that they have been produced to an agreed quality standard.

Warehousing

Higher

Warehousing

Most manufacturing or retailing organisations have to store stock. Finished goods are stored in a warehouse until they are dispatched to the customer. Some organisations have centralised warehouses in which all stock is held before being dispatched. Other organisations have decentralised warehouses where stock is held in smaller quantities at more locations, closer to the customer, before being dispatched. The type of storage used depends on the type of stock to be held, the finance available for storage, company policy, and the number, size and location of customers to be supplied.

Distribution/logistics

This aims to ensure that the right goods are in the right place in the right quantities at the right time to be sold. The correct channel of distribution must be chosen to ensure this occurs (see page 66).

The route through which a manufacturer distributes products is known as the **distribution mix**. This depends on:

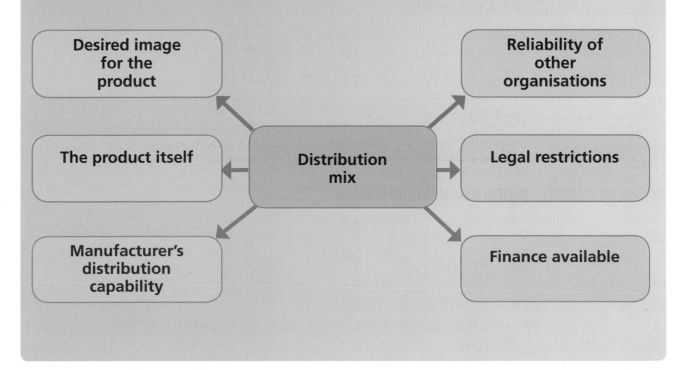

Products can be distributed via:

Road
Road freight (goods transported by road) accounts for approximately 80% of goods transported from one destination to another in the UK. The average freight journey is approximately 50 miles. Most foodstuffs and consumer goods are transported via road. Modern transport vehicles are often designed to transport particular goods (e.g. refrigerated vehicles transport perishable goods; car transporters are specially designed to transport cars). With an ever improving motorway network, road transport can be quick, efficient and cost-effective to use. It allows door-to-door delivery to and from any location, 24 hours a day.

Rail
The quantity of rail freight halved from the 1980s to the 1990s. It has since gradually increased due to increased transportation of coal and other fuel. Rail freight has increased due to specialised rail freight terminals being built, a shortage of lorry drivers, restrictions on the number of hours a lorry driver can work and increasing road congestion. It is more environmentally friendly than road transport. Products arriving at a rail terminal still require road haulage to their final destination.

CASE STUDY

ASDA have decided in recent years to make more use of the rail network for transporting products from distribution centres in England into Scotland. They have taken thousands of lorries off the roads by making increased use of rail freight. They have been striving to cut costs from the delivery chain as road haulage costs have increased.

Marks & Spencer, **Argos** and **Superdrug** also make considerable use of rail freight.

Air
Air freight accounts for a relatively low proportion of goods transported. Prestwick Airport has the largest quantity of freight traffic in Scotland. Transporting products by air is relatively expensive. Products arriving at an airport often also require road haulage to their final destination. Custom-made electronic products that require quick delivery overseas, are often transported by air.

Sea
Scotland's premier ports are located on the Forth Estuary. The main products/freight transported via sea in Scotland are petrol products, minerals and coal. Sea transport is useful for importing or exporting bulky products, but delivery times can be lengthy.

Scheduling

A production plan or schedule is often drawn up to show the order of production, what staff and materials are required and when they are required for. This should eliminate staff and machines being idle whilst waiting for the previous stage of production to be completed.

Quick Questions

1 Why would a business use job production?
2 What influences a business' choice of production method?
3 What is meant by capital-intensive production?
4 Give two disadvantages of labour-intensive production.
5 What is a method study and what is work measurement?
6 What are benchmarking and quality control?
7 Give a brief explanation of quality management.
8 Name the distribution methods a business could use.
9 Why has there been an increase in retailers using rail freight?
10 Why is scheduling important?

Extended Response Questions

INTERMEDIATE 2

1 A small baker has to purchase raw materials to use when baking
bread, scones and cakes. *Describe* the factors that the baker
should take into account when deciding on a suitable supplier. (4 marks)

2 *Explain* why it is important to control stock levels. (3 marks)

3 A manufacturer can choose to manufacture products by job,
batch or flow production. *Describe* each of these *giving* an
example of a product that could be produced using each method.
Give an advantage and a disadvantage of each. (12 marks)

4 *Suggest* an alternative to manufacturing a product using a great
deal of staff input. *Describe* the benefits the alternative you have
mentioned would have. (4 marks)

5 *Explain* why it is important for a manufacturer to ensure that their
products are produced to a high quality standard. (2 marks)

6 *Identify* and *describe* three techniques that could be used by a
manufacturer to ensure that products produced are of
appropriate quality. (6 marks)

HIGHER

1 *Explain* the consequences for a business if they exceed their
maximum stock level or fall below their minimum stock level for
an item of stock. (8 marks)

2 The Managing Director states at the Board of Directors meeting:
'we have kept too much stock, we have high waste and theft –
we must address this problem to remain competitive'. *Identify* a
solution to this problem. *Justify* your choice of solution. (4 marks)

3 The Scottish Parliament building in Edinburgh is unique in its
design and construction. *Describe* the method of production used
to build the Scottish Parliament. *Give* reasons why the architect
and construction company used this method and *give* the
disadvantages that this method presented. (7 marks)

4 *Describe* the advantages and disadvantages to a manufacturer
of manufacturing a product that has been produced using flow
production. (4 marks)

5 *Discuss* the different methods that businesses use to transport
their goods. *Give* an example of when each would be appropriate
to use. (12 marks)

Role and Importance of Finance

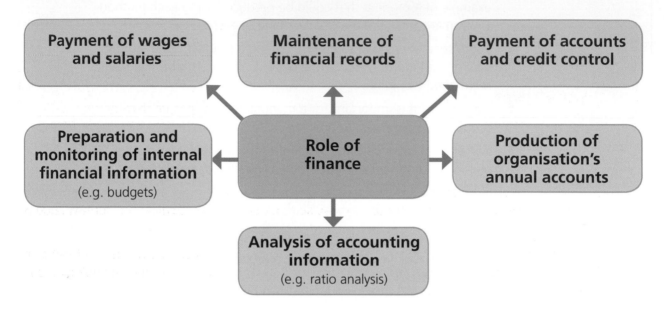

Financial management is vital for an organisation to meet its objectives. Financial information has a number of very important uses to an organisation.

To control costs and expenditure

Financial information allows managers to identify where costs/expenses have increased in order to help them take corrective action.

To monitor cash flow

A business may be very profitable but have poor cash flow resulting in poor liquidity and business failure. A business will pay close attention to cash flow to ensure that it has enough funds coming in to pay bills as they arise. Producing cash budgets assists with this.

To forecast trends

Managers analyse the firm's annual accounts over several years to help them plan likely future costs, revenue and profits.

To monitor performance

Managers use the firm's annual accounts to assess how the firm has performed compared to previous years and competitors. This allows corrective action to be taken if problems are spotted.

To inform decision making

Financial information allows budgets to be prepared for internal uses. Budgets assist with decision-making and planning. Using ratio analysis allows an organisation to decide where improvements need to be made.

Financial records provide information on transactions undertaken by an organisation. This information is gathered together and presented in annual financial statements, in the standard form of a Trading, Profit and Loss Account and a Balance Sheet. All public limited companies must provide annual accounts by law. Scottish-based private limited companies must provide Companies House in Edinburgh with a copy of their annual accounts.

A firm's annual accounts provide a good guide to the profitability, liquidity and efficiency of the firm. A variety of groups and individuals use annual accounts (see users of Financial Information, page 96).

However, its annual accounts may be difficult to compare accurately with another firm's accounts because each firm may use different methods to measure stock values and calculate the current value of fixed assets.

It is important to note that items which are not shown in the annual accounts have a major influence on the performance of the organisation. These include: the morale of the workforce; the technology used; the competition; the stage of each of the firm's products in their life-cycles.

Trading, profit and loss account

This shows the profit or loss over a period of time (normally one year). It identifies how much money has come in to the firm (income) and how much money has been spent and on what (expenditure).

Trading account

Calculates the gross profit or loss (i.e. the difference between the cost to the firm to buy the goods and the sales value of them). Excludes the firm's internal expenses.

Profit and loss account

Calculates the net profit or loss (the profit or loss made after all of the firm's expenses have been deducted from the gross profit).

Trading, Profit and Loss Account of Company X		
Year Ending 'date'		
	£000	£000
Net Sales		100
Less Cost of Goods Sold		
Opening Stock	20	
Add Purchases	50	
	70	
Less Closing Stock	15	
Cost of Goods Sold		55
GROSS PROFIT		45
Less Expenses		
Rent	3	
Advertising	5	
Electricity	1	
Telephone	10	
Wages	3	22
NET PROFIT		23

A partnership and a company also have an **appropriation account** (given after the net profit) which shows how much of the net profit has been distributed among partners or shareholders.

Balance sheet

This shows the value of a business at a particular date.

Items which the business owns and will keep for more than one year. {

Items which the business owns and will keep for less than one year. {

Items which the business owes and will pay for in the short term. {

Shows how the business has been financed. {

Balance Sheet of Company X as at 'date'

	£000	£000
FIXED ASSETS		
Equipment		40
Vehicles		30
Premises		100
		170
CURRENT ASSETS		
Stock at year end	15	
Debtors	30	
Bank/Cash	30	
	75	
Less Current Liabilities		
Creditors	15	
Working Capital		60
		230
Financed by		
Opening Capital		160
Add Net Profit		23
Less Drawings		−3
		180
Bank Loan		50
		230

Debtors are customers who have received goods from the firm but have not yet paid for them.

Creditors are suppliers who have sold goods to the firm on credit and to whom the firm owes money.

Working capital is the difference between current assets and current liabilities. This shows the funds available after short-term debts are met.

Capital is the investment that the owner has put into the firm.

Net profit is the profit made after all business expenses. Tax to be paid is calculated on this figure.

Drawings are funds taken out by the owner from the firm for her/his own personal use.

Ratio Analysis

Annual accounts can be analysed to highlight an organisation's:

profitability – to show how profitable the organisation is

liquidity – to show a business' ability to pay short-term debts

efficiency – to show how efficiently and effectively the organisation is performing.

Ratio analysis is used to:

- compare current performance with that of previous years
- compare performance with that of similar organisations
- identify differences in performance to help decide on future action
- highlight trends over a period of time.

Limitations of ratio analysis:

- information contained in annual accounts is historical as it relates to last year's trading
- inter-firm comparisons must be made with firms of similar size and in the same type of industry
- findings may not take into account external PESTEC factors
- findings do not show the implications of product developments or declining products
- findings do not reveal elements such as staff morale or staff turnover.

Profitabilty/performance ratios

Ratio and formula	Purpose
Gross Profit Percentage $\dfrac{\text{Gross Profit}}{\text{Net Sales}} \times 100$	Measures the profit made from buying and selling stock. If the Gross Profit Percentage needs to be improved, a business may: • increase its selling price • find cheaper suppliers • try to negotiate discounts from exisiting suppliers • increase supervision to reduce theft or breakages of stock.
Mark-up Ratio $\dfrac{\text{Gross Profit}}{\text{Cost of Goods Sold}} \times 100$	Measures how much has been added to the cost of the goods as profit. If the Mark-up Ratio needs to be improved, a business may: • try to negotiate discounts from existing suppliers • find cheaper suppliers • raise the selling price of their products.
Net Profit Percentage $\dfrac{\text{Net Profit}}{\text{Net Sales}} \times 100$	Measures the profit made after the business has paid all business expenses. If the Net Profit Percentage needs to be improved, a business may: • try to improve their gross profit percentage • identify any expenses that can be reduced.
Return on Capital Employed $\dfrac{\text{Net Profit}}{\text{Opening Capital}} \times 100$	Measures the return on the capital invested in the business by the owner or shareholder. The owner or shareholder (i.e. the investor) should compare the Return on Capital Employed with the return offered by other investment opportunities.

Hint

You will not be asked to calculate ratios in the Higher exam. However, it may help your understanding of the ratios if you are able to calculate them.

Ratio and formula	Purpose
Current Ratio/Working Capital Ratio $$\frac{\text{Current Assets}}{\text{Current Liabilities}}$$ Shown as **answer: 1**	Shows the ability of a business to pay its short-term debts. An answer of 2:1 is regarded as generally acceptable. If the Current Ratio needs to be improved, a business may try to increase its current assets or seek ways to decrease current liabilities. The Current Ratio can be too high. A high bank figure may mean that funds could be better employed in the business to generate income rather than sitting in the bank.
Acid Test Ratio $$\frac{\text{Current Assets} - \text{Stock}}{\text{Current Liabilities}}$$ Shown as **answer: 1**	Shows the ability of a business to pay its short-term debts in a crisis situation. Stocks are removed from current assets as it cannot be guaranteed that they can be quickly sold to generate cash to pay off debts. An answer of 1:1 is regarded as generally acceptable.

Cash Flow Statements

Higher

An organisation can show a healthy profit but have poor cash flow leading to problems paying debts on time and paying dividends. A cash flow statement is produced by a company in addition to the trading, profit and loss account and balance sheet to show the movements of cash into and out of an organisation **over the past year**. A company produces a cash flow statement for inclusion in its published accounts that shareholders receive.

Financial Reporting Standards 1 (FRS 1) produced by the Accounting Standards Board provide a layout for producing a cash flow statement. The layout is shown opposite.

Cash Flow Statement for year ended 'date'		
	£000	£000
Net Cash Flow from Operating Activities		600
Servicing of Finance		
Preference Dividends Paid	(40)	
Debenture Interest Paid	(60)	(100)
Taxation		(150)
Capital Expenditure & Financial Investment		
Purchase of Fixed Assets (Equipment)	(120)	
Sale of Fixed Assets (Delivery Vans)	20	(100)
Equity Dividends Paid		(100)
Funds Flow before Financing		150
Financing		
Ordinary Share Issue		200
Increase in Bank and Cash		350

Items with brackets indicate cash going out of the business. Items without brackets indicate cash coming into the business.

Cash Budget/Cash Flow Forecast

A cash budget (also called a cash flow forecast) is produced for internal use within an organisation. It is a **forecast** of receipts and payments of cash. It can be produced for a few months or for a year. It should not be confused with a cash flow statement (see page 94) which is produced for external use based on past events.

A cash budget can be used to:

- highlight periods when a negative bank/cash balance is expected. This allows appropriate finance to be arranged in advance
- forecast surplus cash available as it may allow a firm to invest in assets for the future
- allow corrective action of anticipated overspending on certain payments
- avoid liquidity problems
- secure a loan from a bank
- make comparisons between actual and projected figures to analyse managers' ability to control and monitor cash flows.

Other budgets

Companies can produce production budgets and sales budgets to plan production and sales. These may provide targets for departments to reach. They assist in co-ordinating production quantities that can be sold and allow sales managers to anticipate the quantity they require to sell. Managers should be involved with budget setting to improve motivation and make targets attainable.

Cash Budget for June and July	June £	July £
Opening Bank/Cash Balance	1000	1300
Receipts		
Cash and credit sales	5000	4000
Commission received	500	400
Rent received	200	200
	5700	4600
Payments		
Cash and credit purchases	3400	3000
Wages	500	800
Advertising	1000	1000
Rent	500	500
	5400	5300
Closing Bank/Cash Balance	1300	600

Cash flow problems

Cash is vital to a firm. Without it the firm cannot exist. Firms can fail for a variety of reasons, one of which is poor cash flow. A firm can appear profitable but have no cash if too many customers purchase on credit and do not pay within the agreed credit terms. The business then has little cash to pay such expenses as wages, bills and insurance.

> ### Hint
> Do not confuse a cash flow statement (page 94) which is a document a plc produces for its external final accounts with a cash budget/cash flow forecast that is for internal use.

Sources of cash flow problems
- Tying up too much cash in stock.
- Allowing customers too much credit.
- Customers not paying within agreed credit terms.
- Borrowing too much finance at high interest repayments.
- Owners taking too many drawings.
- Purchase of capital items (e.g. equipment).
- Low sales.

Resolving a cash flow problem
- Offer discounts and promotions to encourage cash sales and reduce stock levels.
- Sell any unnecessary fixed assets.
- Encourage overdue customers to pay their bills.
- Arrange credit with suppliers.
- Seek another source of finance (e.g. find a partner).
- Owners draw less.
- Purchase cheaper products.
- Purchase capital items on hire purchase.

Users of Financial Information

There are a variety of individuals, groups and organisations that use an organisation's financial information. These include:

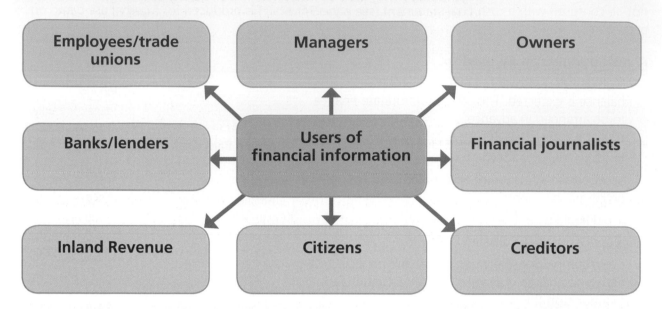

User	Interest in organisation's financial information
Managers	Managers use profitability ratios to check on the organisation's performance in comparison to previous years and competitors. They seek ways to improve the profitability of their organisation for the future. They attempt to identify areas where savings could be made and costs reduced.
Owners	Owners are interested in the profitability ratios, especially the Return on Capital Employed. They compare the return from their investment with other investment opportunities. They can then decide whether to remain as an investor, increase or reduce their investment.
Creditors	Creditors are interested in the overall profitability of an organisation. They are especially interested in the liquidity ratios to assess the likelihood of receiving payment for goods they have supplied or intend to supply to an organisation.
Employees/trade unions	Employees and trade unions assess the profitability of an organisation in order to determine suitable wage/salary increases that they may be entitled to. They may also be interested in the liquidity and sales revenue of the organisation to assess their own and their members' job security.
Citizens	If an organisation is in trouble financially and closes down, the economy of the local community (especially employment) will be severely affected. Local citizens will therefore be interested in an organisation's profitability to ensure continued employment and local economic growth.

User	Interest in Organisation's Financial information	
Banks/lenders	Banks and other lenders assess the overall profitability of an organisation. They are also interested in the liquidity of an organisation to decide whether to supply finance or demand repayment of amounts already loaned. They will also analyse the existing level of debt the organisation has.	
Inland Revenue	This government department is especially interested in the profit made by an organisation. This allows the Inland Revenue to calculate tax due from the organisation.	
Financial jounalists	These journalists use the annual accounts and any other information about an organisation to assess its performance, for inclusion in the financial pages of the national newspapers.	

Sources of Finance

See Sources of Finance, page 19–21.

Quick Questions

1. What is the role of the finance function in an organisation?
2. What use is financial information to an organisation?
3. Define the terms profitability, liquidity and efficiency.
4. Name seven ratios that could be calculated.
5. What is the purpose of each ratio?
6. Explain the purpose of a cash budget.
7. List five ways in which a business can develop a cash flow problem.
8. Name five users of financial information.
9. What interest would a manager and a creditor have in an organisation's financial information?
10. Name five sources of finance an organisation could use.

Extended Response Questions

INTERMEDIATE 2

1. *Explain* why the following financial documents are prepared:
   Trading, profit and loss account; balance sheet;
   cash flow forecast. (6 marks)

2. *Explain* why ratio analysis is used. (3 marks)

3. *Distinguish* between the Current/Working Capital Ratio and the
   Acid Test Ratio. (2 marks)

4. *Suggest* ways in which a business can overcome cash
   flow problems. (4 marks)

5. Managers use financial information to check an organisation's
   performance year-on-year. *Identify* two other users of financial
   information and *describe* their interest in an
   organisation's finances. (4 marks)

HIGHER

1. A potential investor in Scottish Power has asked their Financial
   Advisor to carry out some ratio analysis to decide whether the
   business is profitable or not.

   i) *Identify* two ratios that the Financial Advisor might calculate and
   describe the purpose of each. (4 marks)

   ii) The Financial Advisor had a word of caution over the use of
   ratios. *Explain* why ratio analysis should not be the sole basis
   used when making investment decisions. (4 marks)

   iii) Potential investors would not be the only individuals or groups
   interested in Scottish Power's results. *Identify* three other external
   users of Scottish Power's financial information and *describe*
   the interest each would have. (6 marks)

2. There is a saying in business 'Cash is King'. Without good cash
   flow a business may fail. *Identify* three reasons why a business may
   have poor cash flow and *suggest* a way that a business could
   overcome each. (6 marks)

Hint
Remember to check your SQA command words on page 6.

Role and Importance of Human Resources

Human Resources (HR) planning is very important to an organisation to enable it to meet its objectives. The HR department should monitor trends in labour markets to identify changing patterns of employment over time. Future staffing requirements need to be forecast to identify whether staff need to be recruited, redeployed or made redundant to meet organisational objectives. They also need to anticipate the skills required for the future to enable them to develop training and development programmes to fill any identified skills gaps.

Objectives of HR

- To recruit and retrain quality staff.
- To train, develop and appraise staff to ensure they are equipped with the skills required to produce the best quality output.
- To manage positive employee relations.
- To ensure safe working conditions.
- To ensure that all staff are treated fairly with regard to equality legislation.

The HR department takes on a number of different roles and functions. These are:

Facilitator role

HR staff must provide or facilitate training to other members of staff in the organisation.

Auditor role

HR staff must monitor and report on how effectively individual staff and departments are following HR policies and procedures.

Consultancy role

HR staff must provide specialist guidance and information to managers on how to deal with particular staffing situations.

Executive role

In this role HR staff assume the role of 'resident expert' in all staffing matters.

Service role

HR staff must provide useful information and to be able to do so must keep up with current legislation and other changes that may affect staff.

Hint

Remember that the role of the HR department has a number of FACES.

Higher

Increase in part-time work

Many organisations operate with a team of core workers who are permanently employed in either full- or part-time positions. When required, temporary, casual workers are recruited. Hotels, shops, call centres and offices often operate in this manner. The figures below show the number of workers in Scotland in full- and part-time employment over a period of twenty years. For many years the number of full-time workers has remained fairly static with a recent increase. There has been a significant rise in those working part-time.

	1985	1995	2005
Full-time workers	1 712 000	1 741 000	1 874 000
Part-time workers	401 000	548 000	605 000

Adapted from the Labour Force Survey, Office for National Statistics

Increase in service sector employment

Traditional manufacturing industries have been in decline for a number of years, in contrast to a significant rise in the service sector (see Sectors of Business Activity, page 9). For example, there has been a 40% increase in the number of staff employed in financial services from 1998 to 2004 in Scotland.

Increase in public sector employment

The number of people employed in the public sector, e.g. in education, health, police, local government administrators, etc. has grown continually in recent years. Approximately 30% of Scottish workers are employed in the public sector – a 10% increase since 1999.

Increase in women working

There are now many more women in full-time employment than ever before. Many employers make special arrangements to make it easier for women to remain in employment by providing flexible hours, job sharing opportunities and child-care facilities.

Increase in homeworking/teleworking

There has been a great rise in the number of workers who now work from home. An increasing number of workers spend part of their working week away from the office and work at home. They communicate with colleagues and clients via email, telephone and videoconferencing. There are also an increasing number of people who run a business from their home.

Recruitment process	used by an organisation to find the best possible applicants for a job vacancy to allow an organisation to meet its objectives.

Identify a **job vacancy**

Conduct a **job analysis**

Analyse the vacancy to be filled by identifying the tasks, duties, skills and responsibilities of the position. This helps to identify the type of candidate that would be suitable for the vacancy. After conducting a job analysis an organisation may decide that the position is no longer required and may not fill the vacancy.

Prepare a **job description**

From the job analysis the organisation can draw up a description of the job vacancy. A job description states the job's title, location, tasks, duties and responsibilities. It can also state the conditions of the post including holiday entitlement, benefits and hours to be worked.

Prepare a **person specification**

From the job analysis and job description a description of the type of person that would be suitable for the post can be drawn up. A person specification can describe the qualifications, experience, personal qualities and interests that an ideal candidate would possess. Characteristics are normally split into those that are essential for a candidate to possess and those that are desirable.

Advertise the job vacancy

A job advert can be drawn up using the job description and person specification.

Internal sources   External sources

Internal sources

Jobs can be advertised internally within an organisation through a staff newsletter, notice, intranet or bulletin board. This method of recruitment is often used when internal restructuring is taking place.

This can be an efficient method of recruitment: the vacancy can be filled quickly; it can enhance company morale if a company is known to promote from within; the employer will know the past record of applicants; and the company can save on induction and training costs.

However, applicants are drawn from a limited pool of potential candidates with no new fresh injection of ideas. Also, as one vacancy is filled, another will require filling.

External sources

External recruitment allows an organisation to appoint someone from outside the organisation who can bring new ideas and experience to a job. It may avoid jealousy that might exist between rival internal candidates.

Newspaper adverts

National or local papers can be used depending on the vacancy. National adverts can be expensive to place but they do reach a wide target audience.

Specialist magazines/journals

For example, teaching posts are advertised in TES (the *Times Educational Supplement*); agriculture-related jobs are advertised in *The Scottish Farmer*. By advertising in such magazines and journals employers can easily target potential candidates with the correct qualifications.

Internet adverts

Vacancies can be advertised over the internet on own company websites or on specialist recruitment websites. However, the advert may only reach a limited number of potential candidates.

Job centre

Local vacancies (e.g. for office, hotel and manual workers) are often advertised in job centres.

Recruitment agency

Potential candidates can register with a private recruitment agency. When an employer contacts the agency with a vacancy to be filled, the agency selects candidates from those registered with it for the employer to interview. The agency will receive payment from the employer when it supplies a successful applicant for the vacancy. This process can save an employer advertising costs and can allow staff to be recruited quickly, especially for temporary posts.

Schools/colleges/universities

Employers may contact educational institutions directly to seek young applicants who have the potential to become assets to the company.

CHILDREN 1ST

JOB DESCRIPTION

Post: Fundraising Administrator

Responsible to: Team Leader, West of Scotland Fundraising

Location: West of Scotland Fundraising Office

Salary: £14,730 – £16,515

Job purpose
- Responsible for the day to day running of the West of Scotland Fundraising Office.
- To be a supportive member of the Regional and National Fundraising Teams and assist with meeting fundraising objectives.

Key tasks

Office administration
- Typing of general correspondence, thank you letters, sending out information.
- Initial contact within fundraising office for telephone enquiries and visitors.
- Checking and distributing mail, email and answer machine messages.

Fundraising support
- Administration for events, corporate campaigns and support.
- Co-ordination of press releases.

Financial
- Production of monthly reports from fundraising database.
- Banking all income and acknowledgement of donations.

General office
- Awareness of Quality Assurance policies of CHILDREN 1ST.
- A commitment to involving volunteers in all aspects of CHILDREN 1ST.

Relationships
- To maintain close working relationships with Central Fundraising.
- To attend administrative national and regional meetings.

CHILDREN 1ST

PERSON SPECIFICATION

Post: Fundraising Administrator

Area	Essential	Desirable
Qualifications	Good standard of education	Secretarial qualification
Experience	High standard of organisational and administrative skills Team-working Excellent communication skills Banking and handling cash Excellent telephone manner	
Skills	Proficient in Microsoft Office Word, Excel, PowerPoint 2003 and Outlook Experience of databases Confident and friendly approach	Desktop Publishing Packages
Other	Ability to prioritise and meet tight deadlines Able to use initiative and work with minimum supervision Ability to adopt a flexible approach in response to new challenges Ability to work with volunteers A commitment to the principles of equal opportunities Driver's licence	

Application forms/CVs and references

Application forms should be checked against the person specification to select suitable candidates for a vacancy. As it is normally impractical to interview all candidates, vetting application forms and references allows a short list of the most suitable candidates to be drawn up.

Testing

Tests can be used to provide additional information as to a candidate's suitability for a position. Attainment, aptitude, intelligence, psychometric and medical tests may be used.

Attainment tests often consist of demonstrating skills. For example, a recruitment agency for temporary office staff may give applicants a word-processing test to complete. The resulting words per minute count will be used to assess their skills against a set standard.

Aptitude tests assess the natural abilities that candidates possess. For example, a candidate for computer chip production may be given an aptitude test that measures her or his nimbleness; a candidate for a financial job may be given a numerical aptitude test. The test often reflects the skills required for the particular vacancy.

Intelligence (IQ) tests measure a candidate's mental ability and may involve assessing a candidate's numeracy, literacy, thinking and problem-solving abilities.

Psychometric tests are personality tests where a candidate's responses to questions are analysed to reveal their personality and traits. There are often no right or wrong answers to questions.

Medical tests Certain employers require candidates to pass a medical before considering them for employment. For example, the army, police service and airlines require a medical to be passed.

Assessment centres

Some large organisations have their own assessment centres where candidates are taken for several days. They may take tests including team building and role-play exercises and be interviewed. Candidates will be monitored to assess their social skills, leadership qualities and personality. Smaller organisations can still ask candidates to participate in similar activities either at their offices or at a hired venue.

Interviews

These are used to gather information from candidates by comparing their responses to criteria that successful candidates should have. It also gives an indication of the personality of the candidate. However, interviews can have limitations if a poor interviewer decides that a candidate is not suitable within the first few minutes and focuses on negative aspects of the candidate.

There are various types of interview:

One-to-one interview   One interviewer conducts all the interviews and selects the best person.

Successive interviews   Candidates have several interviews with different interviewers.

Panel interviews   Several people will sit on a panel and the candidate has one interview conducted by the whole panel with each panel member asking questions about different aspects of the job.

The most suitable candidate is selected, offered the position in writing and given a start date.

Unsuccessful applicants are informed.

HBOS' (Halifax Bank of Scotland) university graduate recruitment scheme has four steps in its selection process.

Applicants are asked to complete an online application form containing personal details, education, work experience and experience in four skills areas that are key to success in HBOS graduate positions. If a candidate meets **HBOS'** criteria they are asked to complete an online psychometric test which also includes numerical and verbal reasoning tests.

If a candidate achieves a certain level in the online test they are given a 30–40 minute telephone interview. Those that pass the telephone interview are put forward for the assessment centre. Here, candidates receive further testing, an interview, group exercises, presentations or case studies.

Adapted from www.bankofscotland.co.uk

Training and Staff Development

Most organisations now require staff to undertake training.

Benefits of training staff

- Staff become more competent at their jobs.
- Staff become more flexible.
- Staff motivation increases.
- Staff become more productive.
- Changes become easier to introduce.
- The organisation's image improves.
- There are fewer accidents.
- There is reduced waste.

Costs of training staff

- Once fully trained, staff may leave for better-paid jobs.
- Financial cost of training can be high.
- Work time is lost when staff are being trained.
- Output is lost when staff are being trained.
- Quality of training must be high for it to have a positive effect.
- After training staff may request pay rise.

Type of training	Description
Induction training	When a new member of staff is recruited, he/she usually undergoes induction training upon starting his/her position. This often covers background information about the organisation, organisational/departmental procedures, meeting colleagues, health and safety and an introduction to the tasks of the job. Induction training is designed to make a new recruit feel comfortable in their job.

Type of training	Description

On-going job training

On-going job training can take place:

- **on the job** – where training is conducted at the employee's normal place of work
- **off the job** – where training is conducted at a different location from the normal place of work such as at the company's training centre, college/ university or training provider's centre. This type of training allows trainees to fully concentrate on their training.

Training methods

Demonstration

The trainee watches a task being demonstrated, then completes it themselves.

Coaching

The trainee is taken through a task step-by-step and helped to improve by a trainer or coach.

Job rotation

The trainee moves around different jobs or departments learning different tasks in each. This is an internal method of training.

Distance learning

The trainee receives a pack of materials to work through at their own pace. The trainee then sends completed work to an assessor to be marked or evaluated. This can be used by the trainee to gain an external qualification.

Staff development

Staff often have an individualised plan of personal targets that they try to achieve over a period of time. The targets are often set as part of an appraisal system. Appraisal is the review of performance over a given time period. From the review, training needs may be identified.

Staff may be set individual targets, and may be given salary increases or bonuses. Staff development allows an organisation to identify staff suitable for promotion and assess the effectiveness of their recruitment and selection process. Motivation and morale should improve as a result of a well managed appraisal process.

Employers also try to ensure they suitably motivate their staff. To do this they may:

- issue bonuses and other financial incentives
- involve staff in profit sharing or share ownership schemes
- include staff in works councils and quality circles
- have regular staff appraisals
- organise team-building and social events
- organise staff training.

1 Name and give a brief explanation of the acronym FACES.

2 Identify ways in which employment patterns have changed in recent years.

3 List the steps in the recruitment process.

4 Why might an organisation want to recruit internally?

5 Identify four external sources of recruitment.

6 Name four techniques that could be used to select the most suitable candidate.

7 What is the purpose of using selection techniques?

8 What topics are often covered during induction training?

9 Describe on and off the job training.

10 Describe what is meant by staff appraisal.

Employee Relations

| **Employee relations** | the formal relationships between employees and employers, which may involve each of their representatives. |

The main groups involved in employee relations are **trade unions**, **employers**, **employers' associations** and **ACAS**.

Employee organisation – trade unions

A trade union is an organisation that represents employees with regard to pay negotiations, conditions of service, dismissal, redundancy and other work-related matters. Different trade unions represent different types of workers. For example, the EIS (Educational Institute for Scotland) represents teachers and the NUJ (National Union of Journalists) represents journalists. The TUC (Trades Union Congress) is a body which is made up of representatives from many of the trade unions in the UK.

Trade unions undertake **collective bargaining** on behalf of employees. If workers were to negotiate individually for pay rises and better conditions they would have little chance of success. Trade unions, therefore, negotiate on behalf of all their members. In representing a great number of employees they have a stronger negotiating position. Agreements between trade unions and employers can take place at a national level where an agreement reached affects all employees in the country, or at a local level where an agreement affects one particular factory or workplace.

CASE STUDY

The Transport and General Workers Union (TGWU) is a very large union with over 835 000 members in the UK. It represents workers in many industries including workers in hotels, supermarkets, farm workers, local government, NHS, construction and manufacturing.

The TGWU offers members access to legal advice and representation for any work-related matters such as discrimination, equal pay, health and safety. It campaigns and lobbies for better pay, conditions and pensions for its members. Through collective bargaining it negotiates with employers.

Adapted from www.tgwu.org.uk

Employers

Employers have a duty to undertake a process of negotiation and consultation with their employees and to keep them informed of changes.

Employers' associations

These are employers' organisations which represents employers during negotiation. For example, local councils can be members of COSLA (the Convention of Scottish Local Authorities) which represents them or gives them advice during negotiations with trade unions.

ACAS (Advisory, Conciliation and Arbitration Service)

This is a service, funded by central government, that assists in disputes where agreement between employees and employers cannot be reached. It offers:

advice to employers, employees and trade unions on matters such as contracts of employment, HR policies, legislation and any other work-related matters

conciliation – at the request of management or unions it can intervene in a dispute and try to encourage a settlement that both parties will accept

arbitration – disputing parties put forward their case and agree to ask ACAS to assess the problem and recommend a course of action to resolve the dispute which both parties agree to abide by.

ACAS is often involved in disputes that are heading towards an employment tribunal. An employment tribunal is a legal court that deals with all work-related disputes including unfair dismissal, discrimination and equal pay cases.

CASE STUDY

The table below shows the number of successful employment tribunal cases in the UK by type of claim and the % that were successful out of all claims of that type lodged with the Employment Tribunals Service in 2004–5.

TYPE OF CLAIM	SUCCESSFUL AT TRIBUNAL	
	number	%
Working Time	9249	75
Unauthorised Deduction of Wages	5314	18
Others	3616	18
Unfair Dismissal	3493	10
Breach of Contract	2414	15
Redundancy Pay	1699	28
Sex Discrimination	299	2
Disability Discrimination	236	5
Race Discrimination	107	3
Equal Pay	20	1
National Minimum Wage	25	10

Most unsuccessful cases were either withdrawn, dismissed by a tribunal or were conciliated by ACAS.

Adapted from The Employment Tribunals Service – Annual Report 2004–5

Positive employee relations can be promoted using negotiation, consultation and arbitration.

Negotiation

This occurs when employees and employers jointly discuss matters that are of concern to them in an attempt to reach an amicable agreement. Negotiation often takes place using collective bargaining and usually involves compromise by both sides. Pay deals and working conditions are often agreed upon through a process of negotiation.

Consultation

When an employer wants to introduce change or new technology, they should consult their employees to ensure good relations continue. Consultation involves employers finding out the views of staff in relation to an issue. New procedures and job descriptions are often agreed through consultation.

Arbitration

When a dispute cannot be amicably reached, an independent arbiter, such as ACAS, may be called in to give an impartial solution to the problem which both parties agree to abide by.

There are various ways to involve workers in decision-making and promote positive employee relations:

Worker directors

Workers are elected by co-workers to sit on the Board of Directors to contribute to discussions. Worker directors have no voting powers or directors' privileges but express or communicate employee views directly to other directors.

Works councils

These groups are set up by an organisation and are made up of an equal number of employees and managers. A group meets to discuss any suggestions for change and any changes being introduced. Any major changes should be discussed at a works council before being implemented.

Quality circles

See Quality circles (page 86).

Industrial Action

Higher

When employees and employers cannot agree on certain issues, industrial action may be taken. Official industrial action has the backing of a trade union whereas unofficial industrial action does not.

Employees may undertake industrial action to force the employer to agree to a particular issue (e.g. a pay rise). Industrial action can result in lost production, losing customers and sales revenue as well as gaining a poor image and reputation. A company's share price may also be affected. Employers may undertake industrial action to make employees lose earnings and weaken their resolve. Employers may also threaten employees with redundancy if they do not agree to their terms.

Employee action

- **Sit in**

  Employees remain at the workplace but do no work.

- **Overtime ban**

  Employees refuse to work overtime requested by employer.

- **Work to rule**

  Employees only undertake tasks stated in their job descriptions.

- **Go slow**

  Employees produce work at a slower rate.

- **Strike**

  Last resort action where workers refuse to enter work. This is often accompanied by demonstrations, marches and a picket line.

Employer action

- **Withdrawal of overtime**

  Employer removes the opportunity for employees to work overtime.

- **Lock out**

  Employees are locked out of the business premises.

- **Close**

  Last resort action where a factory or workplace is closed and relocated. This results in redundancy for the existing workforce.

Legislation

Equality legislation
- Equal Pay Act 1970
- Sex Discrimination Act 1975
- Race Relations Act 1976
- Disability Discrimination Act 1995
- Employment Equality Regulations:
  - Religion or Belief 2003
  - Age 2006

National Minimum Wage Regulations 1999

Legislation

Health and safety legislation
- Offices, Shops and Railway Premises Act 1963
- Health and Safety at Work Act 1974

Employment Rights Act 1996

Legislation	Description
Equality legislation	*Equal Pay Act 1970* This states that all employees should receive the same rate of pay where work of 'equal value' is undertaken. Jobs do not need to be identical but require the same skills, expertise and qualifications to be regarded as of 'equal value'. Equality in bonuses, holidays, sick leave and other benefits must also be maintained.

CASE STUDY

The Equal Pay Act 1970 does not define what is meant by the term 'equal value' but the Act generally refers to it being determined by considering the demands made by jobs in terms of effort, skill and decision-making. Despite the Equal Pay Act there is still a large discrepancy between the earnings of women and men as shown in the table below.

	FULL-TIME EARNINGS 2005		
	Women	*Men*	*Pay Gap*
Hourly rates for full-time	£9.82	£11.31	13%
Weekly full-time earnings	£370	£472	21%
Annual full-time earnings	£19,400	£25,100	22%

Adapted from ONS (2005) Annual Survey of Hours and Earnings 2005

Each of the following pieces of legislation makes it unlawful to discriminate regarding recruitment, promotions, terms of conditions of employment and dismissal.

Sex Discrimination Act 1975
This prohibits discrimination on the grounds of sex or marital status.

Race Relations Act 1976
This prohibits discrimination on the grounds of race, colour, nationality or ethnic origin.

Disability Discrimination Act 1995
This prohibits discrimination against disabled persons. Employers have a duty to make reasonable adjustments to the workplace to accommodate staff with disabilities.

Employment Equality Regulations
Employment Equality (Religion or Belief) Regulations 2003
Prohibits discrimination, harassment or victimisation on the grounds of religion or belief.
Employment Equality (Age) Regulations 2006
Prohibits discrimination, harassment or victimisation on the grounds of age.

Employment Rights Act 1996	This states a wide range of duties and rights of an employer and employee. It includes the right of an employee to a written Contract of Employment within two months of starting work which should state the employees job title, working hours, wage/salary details, holidays, pension scheme and date started. The Act also states the right to an itemised pay slip and rights of employees regarding Sunday working, maternity leave and termination of employment.

Legislation	Description
Offices, Shops and Railway Premises Act 1963	This states some basic health and safety regulations that employers must meet regarding minimum: ● working temperatures ● toilet and washing facilities ● first aid provision ● space requirements for staff ● outdoor clothes storage ● cleanliness.
Health and Safety at Work Act 1974	This law added to the Office, Shops and Railway Premises Act 1963 by stating employees' duties with regard to health and safety as well as those of employers. Employees now have a duty to take reasonable care of their own health and safety as well as other employees'.
National Minimum Wage Regulations 1999	This states the minimum wage rates that must be paid to employees. There are three hourly rates, one for 16–17 year olds, one for 18–21 year olds and another for workers aged 22 or over.

Quick Questions

1 Identify the organisations involved in employee relations.

2 What is collective bargaining?

3 What is the role of ACAS?

4 In what ways can positive employee relations be encouraged?

5 Describe a works council and a quality circle.

6 List the action that employees can take if they are unhappy with their employer's actions.

7 Identify three pieces of equality legislation.

8 Identify two pieces of health and safety legislation.

9 How does the Health and Safety at Work Act 1974 differ from the Offices, Shops and Railway Premises Act 1963?

10 What does the National Minimum Wage Regulations 1999 state?

Extended Response Questions

INTERMEDIATE 2

1a *Explain* why a business may decide to recruit staff from outwith the business rather than make internal appointments. (2 marks)

1b *Suggest* three places where a job advert could be placed to attract external applicants. (3 marks)

2 *Explain* why it is important for an organisation to train its staff. (4 marks)

3 *Outline* the details that should be included in a Contract of Employment. (4 marks)

4 *Identify* and *describe* four pieces of employment legislation that an employer must abide by when recruiting and selecting staff. (8 marks)

HIGHER

1 *Describe* the changes that have taken place in the labour market over recent years. (4 marks)

2 *Describe* the steps that an organisation wishing to recruit and select the best member of staff possible would undertake. (8 marks)

3 *Discuss* the value of training staff. (6 marks)

4 *Define* the term 'appraisal'. *Explain* three benefits of appraisal for an employee. (4 marks)

5 *Describe* the measures that an organisation can take to overcome a poor relationship with employees. (8 marks)

6 An organisation is holding a training course on 'HRM Legislation'. *Identify* three pieces of legislation that could be covered in the training course. *Outline* the main features of each piece of legislation chosen. (6 marks)

Hint

When asked to 'discuss' remember to present both sides of the case.

KEY TERMS

Write the following list of key terms and find their definition in the text.

1 Business in Contemporary Society

Asset stripping	Franchisee	Privatisation
Bank loan	Franchiser	Profit maximisation
Bank overdraft	Grant	Public corporation
Board of Trustees	Growth	Public sector organisations
Business Gateway	Hire purchase	Retained profit
Careers Scotland	Horizontal integration	Scottish Enterprise
Central government	Internal growth	Scottish Chamber of Commerce
Charity	Leasing	Secondary sector
Competitive factor	Local authority	Shareholder
Conglomerate integration	Management buy-in	Social and ethical responsibility
Debentures	Management buy-out	Social factor
De-integration	Managerial objectives	Sole trader
De-merger	Multinational	Stakeholder
Divestment	Objective	Survival
Downsizing	Outsourcing	Technological factor
Economic factor	Partnership	Tertiary sector
Enterprise	PESTEC	Trade credit
Entrepreneur	Plc	Venture capital
EU	Political factor	Vertical backward integration
Factoring	Primary sector	Vertical forward integration
Factors of production	Princes Youth Trust	Voluntary organisation
Franchise	Private limited company	

2 Business Information and ICT

CAD	Interactive DVD	Quantitative information
CAM	Internal information	Secondary information
Database	LAN	Sources of information
Data Protection Act 1998	Numerical information	Spreadsheet
DTP	Oral information	Types of information
E-commerce	Pictorial information	Video-conferencing
External information	Primary information	WAN
Graphical information	Qualitative information	Written information

3 Decision-Making in Business

External constraints	Operational decision	SWOT
Internal constraints	POGADSCIE	Tactical decision
Mission statement	Strategic decision	

4 Internal Organisation

Centralised structure

Chain of command

Corporate culture

Customer grouping

Decentralised structure

Delayering

Downsizing

Empowerment

Entrepreneurial structure

Flat structure

Functional departments

Functional grouping

Functional relationship

Hierarchical structure

Informal relationship

Lateral relationship

Line relationship

Line/staff grouping

Matrix structure

Organisation chart

Place/territory grouping

Product/service grouping

Span of control

Staff relationship

Technology grouping

5 Marketing

Advertising media

ASA

Brand

Boston Matrix

Chain store

Channel of distribution

Competitive pricing

Consumer audit

Consumer market

Contribution pricing

Cost-plus pricing

Department store

Desk research

Destroyer pricing

Differentiated marketing

Direct mail

Discount store

EPOS

Extension strategy

Field research

Focus group

Hall test

Independent store

Industrial market

Into the pipeline promotions

Loss leader

Mail order

Market growth

Marketing mix

Market orientation/market led

Market research

Market segmentation

Market share

Market skimming

Merchandising

Niche market

Out of the pipeline promotions

Own label

Penetration pricing

Personal interview

Personal selling

Place

Postal survey

PR

Premium pricing

Price

Price discrimination

Product

Product endorsement

Product life cycle

Product line

Product orientation/product led

Product placement

Product portfolio

Promotion

Promotional pricing

Quota sampling

Random sampling

Socio-economic group

Stratified random sampling

Supermarket

Telephone survey

Test marketing

Trades Description Act 1968

Undifferentiated marketing

Wholesaler

6 Operations

Air freight

Batch production

Benchmarking

Bonus rates

BSI

Capital-intensive production

Centralised storage

Channel of distribution

Commission

Decentralised storage

Distribution mix

Economies of scale

Flat rates

Flow production

JIT

Job production

Kanban

Kitemark

Labour-intensive production

Lead time

Maximum stock level

Method study

Minimum stock level

Overtime

6   Operations—cont'd

Piece rates
Purchasing
Purchasing mix
Quality
Quality assurance
Quality circles
Quality control
Rail freight

Raw materials
Re-order level
Re-order quantity
Road freight
Scheduling
Sea freight
SREDIM
Stock

System design
System operation
Time rates
TQM
Work measurement
Warehouse

7   Financial Management

Acid Test Ratio
Annual accounts
Appropriation account
Balance sheet
Capital
Cash budget/cash flow forecast
Cash flow statement
Creditors
Current assets
Current liabilities

Current Ratio
Debtors
Drawings
Efficiency
Finance
Fixed assets
FRS 1
Gross Profit Percentage
Liquidity
Net Profit Percentage

Profitability
Profit and loss account
Rate of stock turnover
Ratio analysis
Return on Capital Employed
Trading account
Trading, profit and loss account
Working capital
Working Capital Ratio

8   Human Resource Management

ACAS
Appraisal
Arbitration
Assessment centre
Collective bargaining
Consultation
Contract of Employment
Disability Discrimination Act 1995
Employee relations
Employer's association
Employment Equality Regulations
Employment Rights Act 1996
Employment tribunal
Equal Pay Act 1970
Equal value
External recruitment
FACES
Go slow

Health and Safety at Work Act 1974
Homeworking
HR planning
Induction training
Industrial action
Internal recruitment
Interview
Job analysis
Job description
Local level agreement
Lock out
Minimum wage
National level agreement
Negotiation
Offices, Shops and Railway Premises Act 1963
Off-the-job training
On-going training

On-the-job training
Overtime ban
Overtime withdrawal
Part-time workers
Person specification
Quality circles
Race Relations Act 1976
Recruitment
Selection
Sex Discrimination Act 1975
Sit in
Strike
Testing
Trade union
Worker directors
Works councils
Work to rule

QUICK QUESTIONS SOLUTIONS

1 Business in Contemporary Society (p 12)

1 Land, labour, capital, enterprise.

2 **Primary sector** – businesses that grow products or extract resources from the ground, e.g. mining, oil extraction, farming, forestry.
Secondary sector – businesses that manufacture products, e.g. factories and construction.
Tertiary – businesses that provide a service, e.g. banks, shops, hotels.

3 Change in customer demand.
Lack of competitiveness.
Increased foreign competition.
Lack of investment.
UK Government policies.
Trade Union practices.

4 A sole trader is a one-owner business.

Advantages	*Disadvantages*
Keeps all profits.	Unlimited liability.
Total control over decisions.	Restricted finance.
Choose own working hours and holiday periods.	No one to share decisions/problems with.
	No one to share workload with.

5 A partnership is a business with between two and twenty partners/owners.

Advantages	*Disadvantages*
Different partners can bring in different expertise.	Unlimited liability of partners.
More finance available.	Profits have to be shared.
Workload shared.	Partners may disagree.
Stronger borrowing power.	New partnership agreements need to be set up if partners change.

6 Partners become shareholders with limited liability.
No new Partnership Agreement prepared if owners change.
Stronger borrowing position.

7 Take advantage of economies of scale.
Avoid import restrictions.
Avoid restricting legislation in home country.
Receive tax advantages and grants from other countries.
Take advantage of cheap labour in low cost countries.

8 A charity is often owned by a trust. It is controlled by a Board of Trustees.

9 Individual and corporate donations.
Government and National Lottery grants.
Profits from own shop/website sales.
Fundraising – raffles, fetes, Chistmas Card sales, etc.

10 Scouts, youth club, sports club, e.g. a curling club, group that organises a small town's gala or fun day.

1 Business in Contemporary Society (p 18)

1 Huge income generated.
Government relieved of responsibility to run and be accountable for the companies.
Desire to increase share ownership.

2 Profit maximisation.
Growth.
Survival (if under threat of takeover).
Social and ethical responsibility.

3 Give three appropriate objectives relative to given charity. Answers could include:
to provide a service to sick children
to relieve poverty
to relieve suffering to animals
to fund research into various medical conditions.

4 Competition, environment, law, political situation, demands of shareholders, owners or society.

5 **Shareholders** – want a business to be profitable to receive high dividend payments and share price increases.
Employees – want good salaries, job satisfaction, security and good working environment.
Managers – want high salaries, bonuses, responsibility and status.

6 **Donor** – decide to donate or not. Large donors can give charity certain conditions to meet for donations.
Customers – can choose to buy or not to buy from the charity.
Employees – influence the organisation through the standard of their work and fundraising ability.
Government – can set legislation affecting operation of charities.

7 To develop a business idea and combine the factors of production to produce a product or service.

8 Most entrepreneurs set up small businesses where they make all decisions about all aspects of the business. As the business grows it may employ staff who can take on some of the tasks the entrepreneur originally carried out, i.e. pricing goods, serving customers, etc. The entrepreneur can then concentrate on the direction of the business and how it can sustain growth.

9 A franchise is a business arrangement that allows one business (the franchisee) to use another business' name and sell its products or services.

10 Reduced risk of business failure.
May receive training and help with administration from franchiser.
Franchiser may undertake national advertising.

1   Business in Contemporary Society (p 28)

1 **Bank overdraft** – facility where the bank allows more money to be taken from a bank account than is currently in it. Short-term source of finance usually to cover shortfall in cash until payments come in to business. Interest is charged on amount of overdraft used.
Bank loan – the bank agrees to lend money for a stated purpose, period of time and amount. Fixed monthly repayments are agreed. Medium-term source of finance. Interest is charged.

2 **Share Issue** – companies can issue new shares to raise finance. Shareholders in return expect a share of profits in the form of dividends.
Debentures – plcs can issue debentures which are long-term loans. Individuals or other companies may loan a plc money in return for a fixed yearly interest payment. The loan is repaid after a specified period.

3 Describe assistance three of the following could give to a new business: Scottish Enterprise and LECs, Careers Scotland, Business Gateway, Local Authority, Scottish Chamber of Commerce, Princes Youth Trust, Trade Association, Bank, Inland Revenue or lawyers/accountants.

4 Can dominate the market/become market leader.
Reduce risk of being a takeover target.
Increase profits.
Reduce risk of failure.
Remove competitor.
Take advantage of economies of scale.

5 **Internal growth** – where a business uses its own resources to open new shops/factories, hire additional staff or develop new products.
Horizontal integration – where two businesses within the same line of business merge together or one takes over another.
Vertical backwards integration – where a business takes over a supplier.
Vertical forwards integration – where a business takes over a customer.
Conglomerate integration – where a business takes over another that operates in a totally different market.

6
Advantages	*Disadvantages*
Outsourced service may be delivered at a higher quality level.	Less control over outsourced work.
May be cheaper to use outsourced service.	Requires clear communication.
Allows business to concentrate on core activities.	
Can use service only when required.	
Can save on equipment and labour.	

7 Ability of staff and management, availability of finance, information and ICT.

8 **P** – Political – UK and EU legislation.
E – Economic – changes in inflation, interest rates and exchange rates.

S – Social – changes in demographic and socio-cultural trends.

T – Technology – changes in ICT.

E – Environmental – impact of events such as floods, storms, pollution, noise.

C – Competitive – effect of competition.

9   **Demographic** – changes in the size and distribution of the population.

    Socio-Cultural – changes in lifestyle and attitudes in society.

10 Increasing significance of multinationals.

    Publicly-funded organisations becoming more business orientated.

    Importance of small businesses.

    Downsizing trend.

    Importance and growth of franchising.

2   Business Information and ICT (p 37)

1   **Primary** – information researched by an organisation for its own purposes.

    Secondary – information gathered from published sources.

    Internal – information taken from an organisation's own records.

    External – information gathered from outwith the organisation.

2   **Quantitative** – information that can be measured and is normally expressed as numbers.

    Qualitative – information that is expressed in words and is descriptive and involves judgements or opinions.

3   To judge whether information is of high quality it should be:

    timely – available when required and up-to-date

    accurate – free from errors

    appropriate for the purpose it will be used

    easy to obtain

    complete – all relevant information included

    concise and to the point

    unbiased

    cost-effective.

4   Helps to monitor and control the business activities.

    Helps with making decisions.

    Helps to identify new business opportunities.

5   Pick three from:

    Network – can be used to share files and software applications.

    Email – can be used to pass internal and external messages, reports, etc. very quickly. Can be used to send promotional information to customers.

    Videoconferencing – can be used to hold meetings with staff in other geographical areas, customers or suppliers without the need for staff to travel.

    Internet – can be used to advertise and sell products or services (e-commerce), purchase raw materials online or access information.

    Interactive DVD – can be used for training staff.

    Computer Aided Manufacture – can be used to control robotic production process.

6   Increased productivity.

    Reduced waste.

    Increased speed of work.

    Improved accuracy of work.

    Consistent quality.

    Labour saving.

    Cheaper and more reliable than labour.

7   Data Protection Act 1998.

8   Pick three from:

    Databases – can be used to store staff, customer and supplier information.

    Spreadsheet – can be used to prepare final accounts and budget reports.

    Word Processing – can be used to generate reports and letters.

    Desk Top Publishing – can be used to produce high quality booklets, reports and adverts.

    Presentation packages – can be used to present training to employees.

9 Job losses due to less staff required when ICT is introduced.
Remaining staff may have to be retrained or have their skills updated.
Email results in less face-to-face contact with colleagues, customers and suppliers.
Staff may be able to work from home.

10 ICT may lead to decentralised decision making.
Additional department may be created, e.g. to accommodate e-commerce.
Redundancies and delayering may result.
Span of control may decrease.

3 Decision-Making in Business (p 42)

1 **Strategic** – long-term decision made by senior management regarding the overall aim and direction of the organisation.
Tactical – medium-term decision made by middle management regarding how the strategic objectives will be met.
Operational – short-term day-to-day decisions made as changes occur.

2 Answers such as the following, using a clothes shop as an example, are acceptable:
Strategic – to increase sales revenue, to become the market leader.
Tactical – stock items that are more fashionable, lower prices.
Operational – to open up another till when queues are too long.

3 POGADSCIE is a decision-making technique that managers can use to ensure they have thought out the issue fully before making a decision. It involves nine steps:
identify the problem
identify the objectives
gather information
analyse all available information
devise possible solutions
select the best solution
communicate the decision
implement the decision
evaluate the effectiveness of the decision and the influence of ICT.

4 Managers have responsibility for running a business.
Organisational success depends on their ability to make decisions.
Keep staff support and keep them informed of decisions made.
Must meet organisational objectives.

5 A SWOT analysis is a technique used to identify all internal strengths and weaknesses and external opportunities and threats relevant to the organisation.

6 No rash decisions are made.
Decisions made taking advantage of a range of information that has been gathered.
Business more likely to consider a range of solutions to a problem.
Ideas should be enhanced as a range of solutions should be analysed.

7 Can be time consuming and slow down decision-making.
Identifying and choosing between a range of solutions can be difficult.
Creativity may be stifled.
Not suitable for all decisions.

8 Lack of finance.
Company policy.
Staff may resist change.
Lack of ICT.
Staff may be unable to handle complex decisions.

9 Political, economic, social, technological, environmental and competitive factors.

10 Ability of managers making decisions, ability to use decision-making techniques, access to appropriate information, level of risk decision-maker will take, personal interest of decision-maker.

4   Internal Organisation (p 52)

1   **Product grouping** – an organisation with different departments to deal with different products.
Place grouping – an organisation with different departments that operate in different geographical areas.

2

Advantages	*Disadvantages*
Each department can give a service that meets its customers' needs.	Greater staff costs.
Customer loyalty can build up due to personal and appropriate service given.	Administration, finance and marketing may be duplicated across different divisions.

3   A business, especially a large business, rarely uses only one type of organisational grouping. A large plc may have functional departments for marketing, finance, HR, operations and R&D. It may have product groupings for different products it sells. For one of the products it sells it may have sales representatives that are split up into sales territories by place grouping.

4   Shows the formal structure of an organisation.
Shows the relationship between staff.
Shows who has authority over who.
Shows who is in charge.
Shows the chain of command and lines of communication.

5   May be queues for manager's time.
Manager may make snap decisions due to pressure to deal with all staff.
Subordinates may make decisions themselves rather than wait for manager's input.
Manager may lose control.
Manager will have less time for planning.

6   Size of organisation.
Technology used.
Market operating in.
Staff skills.
Products/services offered.

7   When a project team is required to deal with a specific task.
Staff with expert knowledge are drawn from different departments.

8   **Line** – a vertical relationship between manager and subordinate.
Lateral – a horizontal relationship between staff on the same level.
Functional – a relationship between a department with a function that benefits the whole organisation i.e. HR and other departments.
Staff – a relationship between an advisor (IT Advisor) and another member of staff.
Informal – a relationship between any staff where they discuss work on an informal basis during work, breaks, social events, etc.

9   Improve communication.
Speed up decision-making.
Empower staff.
Reduce wage/salary costs.
More responsive to change.

10   Improve staff motivation and productivity.
Improve pay and training for staff.
Provide better promotion prospects.
Faster decision-making.
Allow staff to develop greater skills.

5   Marketing (p 63)

1   Marketing helps to:
raise awareness of products/services
raise the organisation's profile
encourage customers to purchase
target new customers and retain existing ones
know what customers want
monitor changing tastes and trends.

2   Socio-economic group, family characteristics, age, religion, occupation, income, gender, geographical area.

3   **Differentiated marketing** – where different products/services are produced and aimed at different market segments.

Undifferentiated marketing – where a product/service is aimed at no particular segment. It will probably be a mass market product/service that is aimed at the whole population.

4   **Personal interview** – face-to-face interview between interviewer and respondent. May take place in the street, a shop or at home.

Focus group – a group of individuals are chosen to attend a group discussion chaired by an experienced chairperson who leads discussion on a particular product/service or topic.

Telephone survey – market researcher telephones individuals at their home to ask them questions.

Postal survey – individuals are sent a questionnaire through the post to their home to complete and return.

Hall test – customers are invited to try a product and give their reaction to it.

Consumer audit – continuous research is gathered into customer buying habits or influence of advertising. Customers are asked to keep a diary to record their habits.

EPOS – use of electronic shop tills to gather information on customers shopping habits.

Observation – the number of occurrences of an event is recorded, i.e. number of users of a local park to justify expenditure on upgrading park facilities.

Test marketing – when a new product is developed it may be available to purchase in a small geographical area to test reaction to the product before a nationwide launch.

5   It is often impractical and too costly to interview every possible consumer.

6   The 4 Ps – price, product, place and promotion.

7
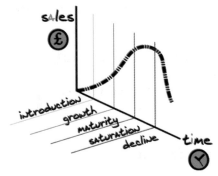

Your diagram should resemble the one shown, although depending on the product you have chosen the height or incline of the curve may be different.

8   Alter the product, packaging, channel of distribution, price, promotion and advertising. Produce line extensions.

9   If a product fails, is overtaken by technology or consumer tastes change the business will have no other products to fall back on to generate profits.

10   **Brand** – a name, logo or design given to a product by the manufacturer.

Own label – a retailer's own product with either the retailer's name or an exclusive own brand. The retailer does not normally produce the product.

5   Marketing (p 74)

1   Company objectives, competitor prices, position on product life-cycle, cost of manufacturing, time of year, level of advertising, profit expected, suppliers' prices, market segment aimed at, place, economy, government pressure.

2   **Penetration pricing** – a product is launched on the market at a low price to tempt customers to purchase the product. Once the product has gained popularity the price is raised to a level in line with competitors.

Destroyer pricing – large businesses can reduce prices to an unprofitable level to force competition out of the market. Once the competition has gone, prices are raised back to a profitable level.

Promotional pricing – prices reduced for a short period of time.

Loss Leader – price of a product may be dropped to a loss making level to encourage customers to enter retail premises where they will then purchase normal priced products.

Competitive pricing – products are priced at similar levels to the competition.

Price discrimination – different prices are charged for different times.

Market skimming – when a new advanced product is launched it is often set at a high price. As competition increases the price will gradually fall.

Premium pricing – a high price is set and maintained to create an exclusive image.

3   Actual product being sold.
Finance available.
Reliability of other companies in the chain.
Desired image for the product.
Government restrictions.

Product's life cycle.
Manufacturer's distribution capability.

4 **Internet selling** – products are sold via the internet.
Mail order – products are sold via catalogues.
Direct mail – promotional leaflets, letters or brochures are sent to customers which can then be ordered via post, telephone or the internet.
Newspaper/magazine selling – adverts are placed in the press and customers can then purchase via post, telephone or the internet.
Personal selling – sales staff visit customers in the home or workplace to explain and demonstrate the product. Orders can then be taken by the sales rep.

5 Often located close to customers.
Established customer base.
Retailer pays for storage, sales staff and premises.
More direct than using a wholesaler.
Offer facilities such as credit, delivery, after-sales service, guarantees.

6

	Benefit	Cost
TV	Target all national market segments. Adverts can be colour, sound and movement. A product can be demonstrated. Maintain high product profile.	Expensive. May not need to reach all market segments. Message can be short lived. Many viewers channel surf when the adverts come on.
National daily newspapers	National exposure. Details can be explained. Products can be aimed at certain market segments depending on the paper. Adverts can be kept for future reference.	People tend not to scrutinise daily newspapers. Only text and pictures available. Can be expensive.
Sunday newspapers	People tend to have the time to scrutinise their Sunday paper. Large national circulation. Supplements printed in glossy colour.	Can be expensive.
Local newspapers	Good for targeting a local audience. Readers scrutinise their paper.	Often slightly poorer quality.
Magazines	Colour adverts create impact. Can target specific market segments. Magazines are often kept.	Can be expensive.
Independent radio	Cheaper to advertise than TV. Listeners tend not to channel surf when adverts come on. Can target particular market segments.	Listeners may not pay attention to the adverts. Relies on listener's imagination. Limited to sound only.
Cinema	Captive audience. Adverts can be shown before particular films to appeal to particular market segments.	Short lived message. Limited audience.
Outdoor media	Can attract a wide audience. Can have a high visual impact. Passers-by see the advert repeatedly.	Weather damage or vandalism. Passers by may ignore it. Can be expensive.
Internet	Relatively cheap. Can target particular market segments. Adverts changed easily.	Web surfers may ignore adverts.
Direct mail	Can target particular market segments.	Customers dislike junk mail. Need to target mail accurately.

7 Advertising Standards Authority.
Trades Description Act 1968.

8 **Price** – the amount the customer pays for a product or service.
Product – the actual item that the customer purchases including the packaging, image, guarantee and after-sales service.
Place – the route the product takes to reach the customer from the manufacturer.
Promotion – the way in which a customer is made aware of a product/service and is persuaded to purchase it.

9 **Into the pipeline promotions** – promotions that are offered by a manufacturer to a retailer.
Out of the pipeline promotions – promotions that are offered by a retailer or manufacturer to the end customer.

10 Organise event sponsorship, charity donations, product endorsement, publicity literature, merchandising and press releases.

6   Operations (p 82)

1 **Purchasing** – decide what, how much and who to purchase from.
System design – decide factory layout, production process, staffing required and degree of automation to be used.
System operation – decide how best to control flow and storage of stocks.

2 Stocks available, time between orders, quantity of raw materials used, storage space available, cost of storage, production spoilage levels, buffer stocks required, finance available.

3 **Maximum stock level** – the level which stocks should not exceed.
Minimum stock level – the level which stocks should not fall below.
Re-order Level – when this level is reached new stock should be ordered.

4

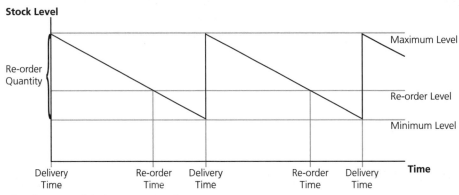

5 Can keep stock balances up-to-date.
Can be programmed to order stock automatically when reorder levels are reached.
Barcodes enable easy checking of stock levels, stock values, best-sellers and slow moving lines.

6 Stock not on hand when required.
Large quantities held may increase deterioration, obsolescence and theft.
Stock held may not reflect actual usage.

7 As stock is delivered just before use there must be effective ordering and quality procedures from suppliers to ensure that stock is received on time every time.

8 Finance not tied up in stocks – improved cash flow.
Less space required – reduced stockholding costs.
Closer relationship with suppliers.
Reduced deterioration, obsolescence, theft or waste.
Less affected by fashion and technology changes.

9 Piece rates, time rates, bonus rates, flat rates, commission, overtime.

10 Piece rates – factory workers.
Time rates – shop and hotel workers.
Bonus rates – financial market workers.
Flat rates – professional workers.
Commission – sales representatives.
Overtime – shop, hotel, factory workers.

6   Operations (p 88)

1 To produce a high quality one-off product exactly to consumer requirements.
   When they want to charge a high price.
   When they want to keep staff motivated.

2 The product being produced.
   Demand for the product.
   Size of the market.
   Size of the business.
   Technology available.

3 Reliance on machinery and automation in the production process.

4 Labour may be expensive.
   Economies of scale limited.
   Production may halt if staff are absent.
   Quality needs to be closely monitored.

5 **Method study** – used to identify how tasks are done to allow a business to develop improved methods.
   Work measurement – used to establish a standard time for completing a task. Staff are then measured against this standard time.

6 **Benchmarking** – a business identifies the best techniques used by competitors. The business then sets out to copy and better competitors.
   Quality control – products are checked at the end of the production process. Raw materials are checked before entering production. This ensures that unacceptable products are not sold to consumers.

7 A system of doing things right first time, all the time. There is zero error tolerance in all aspects of the business from administration to production.

8 Road, rail, air and sea.

9 Increased number of specialised rail freight terminals.
   Shortage of lorry drivers.
   Restrictions on hours lorry drivers can work.
   Road congestion.
   Environmentally friendly.

10 To ensure that production materials are available when required.

7   Financial Management (p 97)

1 Prepare and monitor internal information, i.e. through the use of budgets.
   Pay wages and salaries to employees.
   Keep financial records.
   Pay accounts and manage credit control.
   Produce annual accounts – Trading, profit and loss account, balance sheet, cash flow statement.
   Analyse accounting information using ratios.

2 Helps to:
   control costs and expenditure
   monitor cash flow
   forecast trends
   monitor performance
   inform decision-making.

3 **Profitability** – how profitable the organisation is.
   Liquidity – a firm's ability to pay short-term debts.
   Efficiency – how efficiently and effectively the organisation is performing.

4 Gross Profit %.
   Mark-up Ratio.
   Net Profit %.
   Return on Capital Employed.
   Current Ratio/Working Capital Ratio.
   Acid Test Ratio.
   Rate of Stock Turnover.

5 **Gross Profit %** – measures profit between buying and selling stock.
   Mark-up Ratio – measures how much has been added to the cost of goods as profit.

Net Profit % – measures the profit made after all expenses have been paid.
Return on Capital Employed – measures the return the owner or shareholder receives on their capital invested.
Current Ratio/Working Capital Ratio – shows a business' ability to pay short-term debts.
Acid Test Ratio – shows the business' ability to pay short-term debts when debts require immediate payment.
Rate of Stock Turnover – shows how many times the business sells its stock over a period of time.

6 Highlight periods when finance needs to be arranged.
Forecast when surplus cash is available.
Allow corrective action to be undertaken on areas of overspend.
Used to secure a bank loan.
Analyse a manager's ability to control and monitor cash flows.

7 Holding too much stock.
Allowing too much credit to customers.
Poor debt collection procedures.
Borrowing too much at high interest rates.
Owner taking too many drawings.
Outright purchase of capital items.
Low sales.

8 Managers, employees/trade unions, owners, banks, Inland Revenue, citizens, creditors, financial journalists

9 **Manager** – want to check on performance in comparison to previous years and competitors with a view to identifying areas for improvement.
Creditor – interested in overall profitability and liquidity to determine how likely they will be to receive payment for goods.

10 Bank overdraft, trade credit, factoring, grant, retained profits, bank loan, leasing, hire purchase, owner's savings, share issue, debentures, venture capital.

8 Human Resource Management (p 106)

1 **FACES** is an acronym that summarises the role of the Human Resources function.
Facilitator role – HR staff must facilitate training to staff.
Auditor role – HR staff must monitor and report on how effectively HR policies and procedures are followed.
Consultancy role – HR staff must provide guidance on how to deal with particular staffing situations.
Executive role – HR staff assume the role of 'resident expert' in all staffing matters.
Service role – HR staff must keep up with current legislation and other changes that may affect staff.

2 Increase in part-time work, homeworking, service sector employment, public sector employment and women working.

3 Conduct a job analysis.
Prepare a job description.
Prepare a person specification.
Advertise the job vacancy internally or externally.

4 The position can be filled quickly.
Morale enhanced.
Employer will know past records of the applicant.
Save induction and training costs.

5 Newspaper adverts, job centres, specialist magazines/journals, internet adverts, schools/colleges/universities, recruitment agencies.

6 Application forms/CVs, references, testing, assessment centres and interviews.

7 To decide on a short list of applicants.
To match candidate skills to job description and person specification.
To make sure that the right candidate is offered the job.
To gather additional information about candidates.

8 Background information.
Organisational procedures.
Meeting colleagues.
Health & safety, fire safety.
Introduction to tasks.

9 **On the job** – training is conducted at the employees normal place of work.
Off the job – training is conducted away from the normal place of work.

10 Review of a member of staff's performance. Used to set targets and training needs.

8 Human Resource Management (p 111)

1 Trade unions, employers, employers associations and ACAS.

2 Unions negotiate on behalf of all members to achieve a stronger bargaining power.

3 It offers advice, conciliation and arbitration.

4 Negotiation, consultation, arbitration, employee representation through quality cicrles, worker directors and works councils.

5 **Works council** – a group of equal number of employees and managers. The group discuss any suggestions for change and any changes being introduced.
   Quality circle – a group of employees discuss how to improve a product or the part of the production process that they are involved in then implement the improvement.

6 Involve TU, sit-in, overtime ban, work to rule, go slow and a strike.

7 Equal Pay Act 1970.
   Sex Discrimination Act 1975.
   Race Relations Act 1976.
   Disability Discrimination Act 1995.
   Employment Equality (Religion or Belief) Regulations 2003.
   Employment Equality (Age) Regulations 2006.

8 Offices, Shops and Railway Premises Act 1963.
   Health and Safety at Work Act 1974.

9 Offices, Shops and Railway Premises Act 1963 states minimum requirements that employers must provide for toilets, heating levels, cleanliness, etc. Health and Safety at Work Act 1974 adds to previous legislation by stating employer's and employee's duties with regard to health and safety.

10 The minimum wage rates that must be paid to employees. There are 3 levels depending on the age of the employee.

1 Business in Contemporary Society

Intermediate 2

1

Type of business	Advantages	Disadvantages
Sole trader	Owner keeps profits. Owner makes all decisions. Owner chooses own hours/holidays. Personal service. Easy to set up.	Unlimited liability. Restricted finance. No one to share decisions with. No one to share workload. Work may stop if owner is ill/on holiday.
Partnership	Partners bring different expertise. More finance available. Shared workload. Stronger borrowing position. Shared decision-making.	Unlimited liability. Profits shared. Partners may disagree. New Partnership Agreement needs to be set up if ownership changes.
Private limited company	Limited liability. Control not lost to outsiders. Stronger borrowing position. Expertise of key position holders.	Profits shared. Legal process in setting up. Restricted finance from shareholders. Must abide by Companies Act. Must lodge final accounts with Companies House – can become available to the public/competitors
Public limited company	Large amounts of finance can be raised. Domination of their market. Very strong borrowing position.	High set-up costs. Have to abide by Companies Act. No control of ownership. Must publish financial accounts.

2

Organisation	Stakeholder	Influence
Plc	Shareholders	Voting for directors. Approving dividend payments at the AGM.
	Managers	Make important decisions regarding hiring staff, product portfolio, etc.
	Employees	Standard of their work and industrial relations.
	Customers	Choose to buy or not to buy. Influence the products and services provided. May recommend to friends/family.
	Banks/other lenders	Can grant or withhold loans, set loan interest rates, or request repayment of loans.
	Suppliers	Can change prices, credit periods and discounts.
	Local community	Petition companies. Can place objections with local authorities over planning applications.
	Government	Grant or not grant planning permission.

	Central government	Produce legislation. Economic policies.
Publicly-funded organisation, e.g. NHS Trust	Patients	Petition the Trust. Can choose NHS or private care.
	Volunteers	Choose to give up their time or not to run volunteer services such as canteens, book and tea trolleys and transporting patients.
	Managers	Make important decisions regarding hiring staff, what patient services to provide, etc.
	Charity donors	Decide to run fundraising events to provide additional services and equipment for hospitals.
	Suppliers	Change prices, credit periods and discounts offered on hospital and nursing products.
	Local community	Petition an NHS Trust or make complaints.
	Central government	Produce legislation. Set standards of care.
	Banks/other lenders	Can grant or withhold loans, set loan interest rates, or request repayment of loans.
	Employees	Standard of their work and industrial relations.

3 An entrepreneur is an individual who develops a business idea and combines the factors of production (i.e. land, labour, capital and enterprise) in order to produce a good or provide a service.

4 A franchise is a business agreement that allows one business (the franchisee) to use another business's name and sell the other business's products or services (e.g. The Body Shop)

i)

Franchisee	*Advantages*	*Disadvantages*
	Franchiser may advertise. Risk of business failure reduced. Training and administration help.	Products, selling prices and store layout may be dictated. Percentage of revenue/royalty must be paid. Contract may not be renewed. Costly to purchase a successful franchise.

ii)

Franchiser	*Advantages*	*Disadvantages*
	Increase market share without heavy investment. Reliable revenue. Risks shared.	Only receive a share of the profits. Profits and reputation dependent on franchisees.

5 **Bank loan** – the bank agrees to lend money for a specific period of time, amount and purpose. Repaid in regular instalments with added interest. Budgeting easy as repayments are fixed.
Leasing – rent vehicles from a leasing company/garage. Vehicles can be updated at end of lease agreement.
Hire purchase – a deposit is made for the vehicles with the balance paid up in instalments with interest added.
Owner's savings – the sole trader can introduce additional capital from their own money to pay for the vehicles.

6 **Political** – UK and EU laws and political decisions that affect a business.
Economic – changes in interest rates, exchange rates and whether there is recession or a boom.
Social – changes in the size and distribution of the population or changes in lifestyle and attitudes.
Technological – changes in new technology that a business has to keep up with or lose consumers, sales and profits.
Environmental – events that influence a business such as storms, floods, pollution or noise.
Competitive – competition can influence such things as products, pricing and customer service.

Higher

1

Partnership		Private limited company
Owned by partners	whereas	Owned by shareholders
There can be 2–20 partners	whereas	There must be a minimum of 1 shareholder
Controlled by partners	whereas	Controlled by a Director or a Board of Directors

2   To reduce crime.
To improve community policing.
To stick to agreed budgets.
To implement national crime prevention campaigns.
To increase numbers of police officers.

3   Answers must relate to the hotel.

Stakeholder	Interest and influence
Customers	Want the best quality service, room, food and facilities at affordable prices. Can choose to stay or not. May recommend the hotel.
Banks	Want to ensure the hotel has funds to meet repayments. Can grant or withhold loans, set interest rates or request repayment of loans.
Suppliers	Want the hotel to be a success to ensure repeat custom. Can change prices, credit periods and discounts.
Local community	Want associated income from visitors staying at the hotel. Can make visitors welcome.
Local government	Want the hotel to provide jobs and pay business rates. Can grant licence for hotel. Can grant planning permission.

4

Source of finance	Description	Justification for use
Grant	Obtained from government or EU.	May be given as an incentive to build new factory in an area of high unemployment. Does not need to be repaid.
Retained profits	Profit kept back from previous years.	No repayments or interest to be paid.
Bank loan	The bank agrees to lend money for a specific period of time, amount and purpose.	Repaid in regular instalments with added interest. Budgeting easy as fixed repayments are made.
Leasing	Rent equipment for the factory from a leasing company.	Can be used when finance is limited. Equipment is changed easily when obsolete. Cost of equipment may be spread over several years.
Hire purchase	A deposit can be made for factory equipment with the remainder paid in instalments.	Cost of equipment may be spread over several years. Company owns the equipment at the end of the HP period.

Share issue	Sell additional shares to existing or new shareholders.	Dividends payable from profits in return for shareholders' investment.
		Large amounts of finance can be raised.
		Finance does not need to be repaid.
Debentures	Loans issued to individuals and/or other companies.	Fixed debenture interest is paid yearly to debenture holders.
		Amount of loan repaid at a set point in the future.
		Large amounts of finance can be raised.
Venture capital	A high fee and part-ownership may be handed over to obtain the finance.	May be used where banks decide the project is too risky.
		Usually used for very large loans.

5 **Scottish Enterprise and Local Enterprise Companies** – government-funded organisations that offer advice, provide contacts, assist with gaining grants and funding, promote exporting.
Scottish Chamber of Commerce – an organisation that businesses can become members of. They encourage exporting and international trade.
Banks – give advice on sources of finance and drawing up a business plan for expansion.
Inland Revenue – gives advice on taxation matters.
Lawyers and accountants – give legal and financial advice.

6i) To avoid being a takeover target.
To reduce the risk of business failure.
To become the market leader and dominate the market.
To expand into a new market area.
To increase profits.
To remove a competitor.
To be able to take advantage of economies of scale.

ii) **Internal growth** – opening up new factory, hiring additional staff or developing new products.
Horizontal – businesses in the same market combining. Buttercreme to combine with another dairy.
Vertical forward – a business takes over a customer. Buttercreme to combine with a retailer.
Vertical backward – a business takes over a supplier. Buttercreme to combine with a farm.
Conglomerate – a business combines with another operating in a different market. Buttercreme to combine with a mobile phone company.

iii) **Economic** – changes in interest rates, exchange rates, effects of a recession.
If interest rates rise or there is a recession consumers may swap to lower cost butters.
If Buttercreme imports ingredients from abroad an increase in the £ means they can be bought for less.

Social – consumers' tastes may change.
May want organic butter.
May want low-fat butter.

Technological – changes in new technology.
New automated production processes may have to be introduced to reduce costs.
A website set up to market products. Use of email to inform customers of products.

Environmental – weather events that influence a business such as storms, floods or pollution and noise.
If a storm prevents milk being collected from farms, no butter can be produced.
If disease, e.g. Foot and Mouth Disease, strikes suppliers, less milk will be able to be collected.

Competitive – competition can influence such things as a business' products, pricing, customer service.
If the competition change their pricing or products, Buttercreme may have to follow suit to remain competitive.

Internal – factors within a business.
Lack of finance may restrict ability to install new technology.
Business may not have accurate market research information leading to poor new product development.

Intermediate 2

1

Primary		Secondary
Information researched directly by an organisation for its own purposes	whereas	Information gathered from published sources
Usually using observation, surveys, questionnaires	whereas	Newspapers, internet and magazines
Gathered from field research	whereas	Gathered from desk research

2

Type of information	Description	Examples of use
Written	Text	Letters to customers. Memos to staff about working conditions. Emails to staff about pay rises. Organisation's information on its website.
Oral	Verbal and sound	Telephone conversations with staff, customers and suppliers. Deliver staff training presentations. Conduct meetings.
Pictorial	Pictures and photos	Include product pictures in catalogues and websites.
Graphical	Graphs and charts	Graphs of sales and profit figures.
Numerical	Numbers	Financial accounts (Trading Profit and Loss Account). Ratio analysis. Cash Flow Forecasts/Cash Budgets.

3 Answers must relate to promoting/selling products.

	Advantages	Disadvantages
Email	Can email a large number of customers with one email. Provides instant communication about product queries. Can reach customers worldwide.	Customers may not check email regularly.
Internet	Website available 24 hours a day, 7 days a week. Can show pictures and movie-clips to advertise products. Costs cut – fewer retail premises and sales staff for internet only businesses.	Technical problems may affect availability of site. Customer unwillingness to purchase from internet.

4

Software	Use	Features
Database	Store staff records	Search/query for specific information. Sort records into orders. Perform calculations within records. Produce reports. Mailmerge with a WP document.
Word Processing	Produce staff reports	Format text.
	Prepare letters to job applicants	Mailmerge with a database. Importing text, graphics, graphs into a document.
Presentation package, e.g. MS Powerpoint	Presentation for staff training	Animate text, graphics, photos, charts. Introduce sound, video clips.

1

Source of information	Benefits	Costs
Primary	Correct for purpose collected. Private. Likely to be up-to-date. Source known.	Research costs may be high. Research may be flawed. Respondents may have lied. Time consuming to collect. Researcher bias.
Secondary	Inexpensive. Easy to access. Wide variety available.	May not be suitable for purpose. Biased. Out of date. Available to others.
Internal	Accurate. Easy to access. Private.	Systems to produce information can be costly. Requires accurate records. Regular updates required.
External	Easy to access. Cheap. Wide variety available.	Time consuming. Out of date. Unreliable or biased. Available to others.

2 **Timely** – up-to-date newspaper must be used to have any value.
Accurate – share prices are quantitative, numerical information taken from the Stock Market. Daily prices given in newpapers will be accurate and reliable.
Appropriate – share price information is appropriate information to use when making investment decisions therefore is valuable.
Available – newspapers are readily available.
Concise – newspaper articles tend to summarise all relevant information so should be concise and valuable.
Complete – not all information about a business will be shown in share prices or mentioned in a newspaper article. The reader should be aware that there are issues such as staff morale and new product developments that are not shown in a share price.
Cost-effective – newspapers are cheap to purchase.
Objective – newspaper reports are one person's interpretation of the facts. May be biased or unreliable.

3

Email to send any computer-based information between Head Office and Malaysia.	Instant communication. Documents can be sent and received 24 hours a day. Cost-effective as email can be cheap to send and receive. One message can be sent to many recipients at the same time. Attachments of reports, pictures and policies can be sent with an email.
Video-conferencing or **webcams** to enable staff at both sites to have meetings where they can see and hear each other.	Saves travel and accommodation costs. No work lost due to travelling. Webcam technology is relatively cheap.

4i)   **ii)**

Effect on employees	Effect on the production process
Fewer staff required. Remaining staff will require retraining. Staff may become deskilled. Span of control may decrease.	Increased productivity. Reduced waste. Consistent production quality. Less staff required. Production safer. Possibility of 24/7 production.

3 Decision-Making in Business

Intermediate 2

1 **Strategic** – long term decisions made by top management regarding the aim and direction of the organisation, e.g. to improve profits, to become the market leader.

Tactical – medium-term decisions made by middle management regarding how to achieve the strategic decision, e.g. decision to conduct market research to find out reasons for falling profitability, decision to open additional stores.

Operational – day-to-day decisions most often made by middle and junior managers but staff at all levels will make operational decisions, normally in response to changes occurring, e.g. to close a store due to flood that happened overnight, to hire additional part-time staff to cover Christmas period.

2 Use decision-making techniques.
Use all available information when making decisions.
Inform staff of decisions.
Ensure decisions are in line with organisational objectives.

Higher

1i) **Tactical** – medium-term decisions made by middle management regarding how to achieve the strategic decision. Hire additional police officers, mount a specific campaign, e.g. a knife amnesty.

Operational – day-to-day decisions most often made by middle and junior managers normally in response to changes occurring, e.g. send police officers to a particular incident, change work rota if a large number of staff are called to court duty.

ii)

Internal	External
Finance/budget restrictions	**Political decisions** – new laws passed by central government.
Available police officers	**Economic** – during a recession crime may rise.
Police practices and policies	**Social changes** – changes in society's views and expectations.
Staff and unions may resist change	**Technological changes** – developments in technology available to police officers make policing more effective.
Police may lack appropriate equipment or technology	**Environmental changes** – weather disasters mean police officers may have to be redeployed.
Police decision-makers may be unable to handle complex decisions	**Competitive** – policies and initiatives that other forces introduce.

2 **POGADSCIE** – use a structured decision-making model using nine steps:
identify the problem
identify the objectives
gather information
analyse the gathered information
devise possible solutions
select the best solution
communicate the decision
implement the decision
evaluate the effectiveness of the decision and the influence of ICT.

SWOT Analysis – use to identify the internal strengths and weaknesses and external opportunities and threats.
Can be used to:
analyse a person, department or product
build on a business' strengths
correct weaknesses identified
take advantage of opportunities
take measures to protect against threats
be proactive rather than reactive.

PEST Analysis – involves analysing the external factors that affect an organisation – political, economic, social and technological.

Brainstorming – a group of individuals meet to solve a problem. Ideas are discussed in turn and used to find creative solutions.

3

Costs	Benefits
Time consuming.	No rash decisions made.
Slower decision-making.	Decisions made using relevant gathered information.
Choosing from options may be difficult.	Time taken to develop a range of solutions.
Creativity stifled.	Ideas enhanced.

4   Internal Organisation

Intermediate 2

1   **Span of control** – number of subordinates working under a superior.
Functional organisation – organisation split into functional departments of marketing, finance, HR, operations and R&D.
Downsizing – removing departments to cut staff and costs thereby increasing profits.
Informal relationships – develop between staff during work, breaks and social events. Staff share work-related information and advice.

2

Tall		Flat
Tall/hierarchical pyramid with many levels	whereas	Low pyramid with few levels
Slow decision-making	whereas	Decisions passed easily to all staff
Employees tend to be specialised in departments	whereas	More independence to departments
Slow communication	whereas	Information passes easily to all staff
Tend to be large traditional organisations	whereas	Organisations tend to be small/medium-sized
Inflexible organisation	whereas	Can respond easily to change

3

Delayering	Fewer levels of management.
	Increased span of control.
	Improved communication.
	Quicker decision-making.
	Empowered staff.
	Costs cut.
	More responsive to market changes.
Downsizing	Costs cut and profits increased.
	Empowered staff.
	More competitive.
	Loss of valuable skills, experience and knowledge.
Outsourcing	Costs cut – less equipment and labour required.
	Can concentrate on core activities.
	Less control of outsourced work.

Higher

1i) Place/territory grouping – staff divided according to geographical area.

ii)

Functional grouping	May be unresponsive to change.
	Self interest of departments.
	Allows specialisation.
	Based on marketing, finance, HR.
	Clear structure.
	Line relationships and chain of command clear.
Product/service grouping	Duplication of staff/tasks/resources.
	Divisions may compete against one another.
	Divisions more responsive to changes in their area.
	Staff develop considerable expertise of their product.
	Management can easily compare performance of different departments.
Customer grouping	Duplication of staff/tasks/resources.
	Divisions able to offer service to suit particular customer needs.
	Customer loyalty built up.

2   Most are small businesses.
Often have one owner and several workers.
Structure will have two or three levels only.
Business more responsive to change.
The owner will make all the decisions regarding pricing, products, hours, etc.
Decisions can be made quickly.
No confusion over who is in charge.

3   Relieves senior managers of routine tasks.
Subordinates more motivated.
Decision-making quicker.
Decisions more relevant to local conditions.
Local managers may not possess high quality decision-making skills.
Training in decision-making may be required.
Decisions made may not reflect organisational objectives.

4   **Empowerment** – giving staff responsibility for their own work and decision-making:
decisions taken quickly
more flexible staff
increased motivation
improved productivity
improved competitiveness
more ideas generated
improved communication.

5 Marketing

1

Field research		Desk research
Information gathered first-hand	whereas	Published sources
Used to gather primary information	whereas	Process used to gather secondary information
Often gathered from questionnaires and surveys	whereas	Information found in newspapers and reports
Source can be verified	whereas	May not know actual source of information
Likely to be up to date	whereas	May be out of date
Information can be kept private	whereas	Information available to all

2

Personal interview – face-to-face interview.		
	Advantages	**Disadvantages**
	Two-way communication. Researcher can encourage responses. Misunderstandings can be cleared up during interview.	Expensive. Home personal interviews unpopular.
Focus group – groups of consumers selected to discuss a product, advertising campaign, etc.		
	Only qualitative information gained.	Difficult to analyse qualitative information.
Telephone survey – market researcher telephones people at home to ask questions.		
	Inexpensive. Immediate response. Large number can be surveyed. Can cover large geographical area.	Customer dislike of telephone surveys.
Postal survey – questionnaires sent through the post.		
	Inexpensive. Large number can be surveyed. Can cover large geographical area.	Questions have to be simple and straightforward. Low response rate. Incentives for return have to be offered.
Hall test – customers try a product and give their reaction to or opinion of it.		
	Only qualitative information gained.	Difficult to analyse qualitative information. Flawed results possible.
Customer audit – selected customers are asked to use a product and keep a diary of their opinions and reactions to it.		
	Accurate if diaries kept properly. Good for highlighting long term trends.	Expensive. High turnover of respondents. Diaries may be inaccurate.
EPOS – shops can use their electronic checkouts to gather information on spending habits of customers.		
	Accurate customer information gained. Can create customised customer promotions.	Expensive equipment required.
Observation – activities are observed and recorded, i.e. number of cars using a road.		
	Accurate quantitative information gained.	Cannot ask questions to explain observations.
Test marketing – a new product is launched on the market in a limited geographical area. Research is then carried out to find out what customers think of the product before a nationwide launch.		
	Can make product changes before an expensive nationwide launch.	One region may not represent entire population.

3

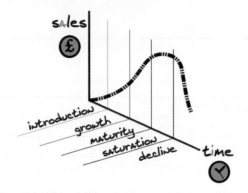

Introduction – product launched, high costs of stock holding, advertising and promotion. Few competitors. High price.

Growth – sales increase. A few competitors may enter the market.

Maturity – product becomes widely available. Growth slows, competition increases, prices fall.

Saturation – fierce competition, prices fall. Customer tastes may change. Some companies cannot survive.

Decline – sales fall, prices very competitive, product withdrawn.

4

A name, symbol, design or combination of these given to a product by the manufacturer.	
Advantage	*Disadvantage*
Seen as a guarantee of quality 'snob value'. Easily recognisable.	High price. Paying for packaging and advertising. May be duped into buying a fake/counterfeit product assuming it is the same quality as the original.

5

	Description	*Example*
Penetration	Product is launched at a low price to tempt customers to purchase the product. Once popular the price is raised to a level in line with competitors.	A new product in an existing market, e.g. a new teenage magazine.
Destroyer	Prices reduced to an unprofitable level to force competition out of the market. Once the competition has gone, prices are raised back to a profitable level.	Used by companies who want to expand into other areas, e.g. bus companies.
Promotional	Prices reduced for a short period of time.	Companies wanting to gain a competitive advantage, e.g. supermarkets.
Loss leader	Price of a product may be dropped to a loss making level to encourage customers to enter retail premises where they will then purchase normal priced products.	Supermarkets and other smaller food retailers.
Competitive	Prices are similar to the competitors. Compete on a non-price basis using advertising, promotions, packaging, etc.	Where competitors do not want a price war, i.e. petrol retailers.
Price discrimination	Different prices are charged for different times.	Companies that often provide a service i.e. telephone providers, public transport or holiday companies.
Market skimming	A new product is launched at a high price. As competition increases the price will gradually fall.	When new, technologically advanced products are launched, i.e. the first plasma screens or DVD players launched.
Premium pricing	A high price is set and maintained. A business wanting to create and keep an exclusive image for its products.	Aston Martin, Rolex, Ray Ban.

6 The product.
Finance available.
Reliability of retailers/wholesalers.
Image desired for product.
Government restrictions.
Product life-cycle.
Manufacturer's distribution capability.

7 Promotional materials sent to individuals or organisations.
Personalised through mail merge.
Target specific market segments.
Cover wide geographical area.
Used to encourage customers to purchase via post, website or telephone.

8

Method of advertising	Advantages	Disadvantages
Independent radio	Cheaper than TV. Captive audience. Target specific market segments.	Non-attention to adverts. Sound only. Reliant on listener's imagination.
Cinema	Captive audience. Target specific market segments.	Short-lived message. Limited audience.
Outdoor media	Wide audience. High visual impact. Often seen.	Weather deterioration/vandalism. Become part of the scenery. Certain forms are expensive.
Internet	Cheap. Target specific market segments. Changed easily.	Adverts often ignored.
Direct mail	Target specific market segments.	Customers dislike junk mail. Customers need careful targeting.

Higher

1 **Product orientation** – company makes a product then tries to sell it; product research and product testing are key; little/no market research done.

Industrial market – the customer is another company not a private individual.

Differentiated marketing – different products/services provided for different customers; makes use of market segmentation.

2 When a product is aimed at a small market segment.

Attractive because: Able to build up expertise in one type of product or customer.
Avoid competition.
Often high price, quality products.

Risks: If successful may attract unwanted competition.
High risk of failure.
Reliant on small number of customers.

3 Market research is the systematic gathering, recording and analysing of data about an organisation's products and/or services and its target market. Businesses spend large amounts of finance on it:
To anticipate changes in the market and customer tastes.
To keep ahead of competitors.
To meet customer needs.
To highlight a gap in the market.
To set correct prices and promotions.
To ensure product is sold in the correct places.
To attract new market segments.
To ensure selling methods are effective.
To find out information about a test product.

4

Random sampling	Individuals pre-selected from a list.
	Interviewer makes calls randomly from the list.
	People selected must be interviewed.
	Limits bias.
Quota sampling	Researcher interviews specific numbers of individuals with particular characteristics.
	Researcher has to find individuals to fit the characteristics.
	Cheaper method.

5 Change the product.
Change the packaging.
Change the channel of distribution.
Change the promotional activities.
Change the use customers have for the product.
Rebrand the product.
Produce line extensions.
Change the price.

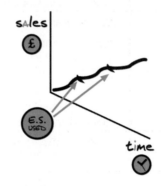

6

Penetration pricing	Product is launched at a low price.
	Once popular the price is raised to a level in line with competitors.
	Used when launching a new product in an existing market.
	Used to tempt customer to purchase the product.
Competitive pricing	Prices are similar to competitors.
	Businesses compete using advertising, promotions, location, packaging, etc.
	When businesses want to avoid a price war.
Market skimming	A new product is launched at a high price.
	As competition increases the price will gradually fall.
	Allows high R&D costs to be recouped.
Price discrimination	Different prices are charged for different times.
	Prices rise during peak periods when demand is greatest.
Premium pricing	A high price is set and maintained.
	Used when a business wants to create and keep an exclusive image.

7 The product.
Finance available.
Reliability of retailers/wholesalers.
Image desired for product.
Government restrictions.
Product life-cycle.
Manufacturer's distribution capability.

Cinema	Advertising before cinema films.	Captive audience. Can target particular market segments.
Internet	Advertise on own website or as banner on another site.	Relatively cheap. Can target particular market segments. Worldwide audience. Adverts changed easily.
Direct Mail	Post promotional materials to customers' homes. Orders can then be placed over the phone, via post or website.	Can target particular market segments. Personalise letters. Cover wide geographical area.
Product Endorsement	Arrange for a celebrity to use its products and appear in adverts.	Customers encouraged to purchase to copy the celebrity.
Product Placement	Arrange for products to be used and seen in TV programmes and films.	Can target specific market segments if placed in the right film. Increases profile of company/products.

9   Into the Pipeline

Point of sale materials – provide stores with posters, cardboard cutouts, shelving to display biscuits.

Dealer loaders – used to attract orders, i.e. buy ten boxes get one free.

Sale or return – allow retailer to return unsold stock after a certain time period.

Credit facilities – allow retailer to buy stock and pay for it at a later date.

Out of the Pipeline

Free offers – encourage customers to buy products by offering free items, e.g. a free storage box could be attached to each packet of biscuits.

Coupons and vouchers – allow customers money off a future purchase, e.g. print vouchers on other McVities products for new biscuits.

Free samples – hand out free samples in supermarkets.

Competitions – have a competition on the back of the biscuit packets.

BOGOFs – display a buy one get one free offer on the biscuits.

Intermediate 2

1   Appropriate quality.
    Can quantity be delivered when required?
    Delivery times.
    Dependability and reliability of supplier.
    Price, discounts, credit terms.
    Location of supplier.

2   Uncontrolled stock can lead to too much or too little stock being held.
    Avoid theft.
    Avoid waste.
    Avoid shortages.

3

Method of production	Advantages	Disadvantages
Job production – used where a single custom-made product is produced, e.g. wedding cakes, bridges, architect designed house.	Can meet exact customer needs. High price can be charged. Specifications can be changed during production. Workers more motivated.	Expensive due to skilled workers' wages. High R&D costs. Wide variety of tools/equipment needed. Lengthy lead times.
Batch production – groups of similar products are produced, e.g. newspapers, bread.	Batches can be changed to meet specific customer requirements. Less need for costly, skilled staff. More standardised equipment.	Special planning required. Expensive machinery needed. High stock levels. Less motivated staff. If batches are small, costs will still be high.
Flow production – mass produced products where items move continuously along a capital-intensive production line, e.g. bottled and canned goods.	Increased economies of scale. Bulk discounts on raw materials. Large quantities produced. Lower costs due to automation. Machinery works 24/7.	High investment to set up. Cannot meet individual customer needs. Inflexible machinery. Low production staff motivation. Breakdowns are costly.

4

Capital-intensive production benefits:	A standard product is produced with standard operations. Little need for expensive labour. Consistency of product and quality. Take advantage of economies of scale. Continuous production.

5   Easier to meet customer demands.
    To meet safety standards.
    To meet legal requirements.
    To ensure the product works properly.
    To be able to charge a premium.

6   **Benchmarking** – improving quality of products, service or production by copying the best techniques used by another organisation regarded as the 'best'.
    Quality Control – checking products meet required standards at set points in the production process.
    Quality Circles – small groups of workers meet regularly to discuss where improvements can be made.
    Quality Assurance – products are checked at certain points in the production process to ensure they meet standards.

Higher

1

Exceed maximum level:	Fall below minimum level:

Exceed maximum level:
High storage costs.
High maintenance costs.
High security costs.
High handling costs.
Large amounts of space used.
Finance tied up that could be used elsewhere.
Unsold stocks can become obsolete or spoiled.
Increased theft.

Fall below minimum level:
Cannot cope with unexpected changes in demand.
If new stocks are delayed stocks may run out.
Cannot cope with shortages of raw materials.
More orders may be required, higher admin costs.
Out of stock costs.
Poor reputation.
Loss of unsatisfied customers.

2

Set a maximum stock level (This is the level that stocks should not exceed.)	Storage costs reduced. Maintenance costs reduced. Security costs reduced. Handling costs reduced. Amount of storage space reduced. Finance tied up reduced. Less obsolescence and deterioration of stock. Theft reduced.
Set up a stock control system with stock cards	Reduced theft. Reduced waste. Reduced stock shortages.
Set up a computerised stock control system	Balances kept up-to-date. Stock levels constantly up-to-date. Computer orders appropriate quantities of stock when reorder levels are reached. Easier monitoring of stock levels.
Set up a JIT system	Finance not tied up in stock. Less stock storage space required. Reduced deterioration, obsolescence or waste of stock. Less vulnerable to changes in taste. Reduction in stockholding costs. Increase in cash flow.

3

Method of production	Reasons used	Disadvantages
Job production – used where a single custom-made product is produced.	Can meet exact customer needs. High prices can be charged. Unique design. Specifications can be changed during production.	Expensive due to skilled workers' wages. Wide variety of tools/equipment needed. Lengthy lead times.

4

Advantages	Disadvantages
Increased economies of scale.	High investment to set up.
Bulk discounts on raw materials.	Cannot meet individual customer needs.
Large quantities produced.	Inflexible machinery.
Lower costs due to automation.	Low production staff motivation.
Machinery works 24/7.	Breakdowns are costly.

Road	Most common method used to transport goods.
	Can use specialised transport when necessary, i.e. refrigerated lorries, car transporters.
	Allows door-to-door deliveries.
	Quick deliveries.
	Allows 24 hours deliveries.
	Causes congestion.
	Shortage of lorry drivers.
	Restrictions on working hours of drivers.
	Not environmentally friendly.
	Used to distribute retail products – foodstuffs, clothes, home improvement products.
Rail	Increasing use of rail freight.
	Specialised rail freight terminals recently developed.
	Environmentally friendly.
	Can transport large amounts of goods.
	Still require road haulage to reach destination.
	Used to distribute coal, fuel, increasingly used by retailers.
Air	Relatively small proportion of goods transported by air.
	Quick method of international transportation.
	Expensive.
	Still require road haulage to reach destination.
	Used when importing/exporting products that require quick delivery – flowers, small electronic products.
Sea	Used to import/export bulky products.
	Lengthy delivery times.
	Used to transport petrol, minerals, coal, grain, vehicles.

Intermediate 2

1

Trading, profit and loss account	To show stakeholders the profit or loss over time.
	To show gross profit – profit made between buying and selling products.
	To show net profit – profit after all expenses.
	Allows taxation to be calculated on net profit.
Balance sheet	To show the value or net worth of a business.
	To show how the business has been financed.
	To show the working capital position of the business.
Cash flow forecast	Highlight when finance needs to be arranged.
	Forecast when surplus cash is available.
	Help avoid liquidity problems.
	Allow action to be taken to reduce spending.
	Secure a loan.
	Analyse a manger's ability to control cash flow.

2   Compare performance with other years.
Compare performance with similar organisations.
Identify differences in performance and decide on future action.
Highlight trends over time.

3

Current/working capital ratio		Acid test ratio
Shows the ability of a business to pay its short-term debts	whereas	Shows the ability of a business to pay its short-term debts very quickly
2:1 is an acceptable figure	whereas	1:1 is an acceptable figure
Total current assets figure used	whereas	Stock removed from the current assets figure

4   Offer discounts and promotions.
Sell unnecessary fixed assets.
Encourage debtors to pay promptly.
Arrange credit with suppliers.
Arrange a new source of finance.
Reduce owner's drawings.
Purchase cheaper products.
Purchase assets on hire purchase.

5

Creditors	Interested in overall profitability.
	Interested in liquidity.
	Want to know if a customer can pay.
Employees	Interested in profitability.
	Want to know if wage rises are likely.
	Want to know job security.
Citizens	Interested in profitability.
	Want to know if organisation will continue to provide employment.
Owners	Interested in profitability.
	Want to know return on their capital invested.
	Allow comparisons with other investment opportunities.

Higher

1i) **Gross Profit percentage** – measures profit made from buying and selling stock.

Net Profit percentage – measures profit made after all expenses.

Mark-up Ratio – measures how much has been added to the cost of goods as profit.

ii) Information is historical.

If making comparisons with other businesses they must be of similar size and in the same industry.

Do not take account of PESTEC factors.

Do not take account of internal factors such as staff morale, staff turnover, new products.

iii)

Creditors	Interested in overall profitability.
	Interested in liquidity.
	Want to know if a customer can pay.
Inland Revenue	Interested in profitability.
	Want to know profits to calculate tax the business should pay.
Banks/lenders	Interested in profitability and liquidity.
	Used to decide whether to grant loans.
	Used to assess ability to pay existing loans.
Citizens	Interested in profitability.
	Want to know if organisation will continue to provide employment.
Financial journalists	Interested in all aspects of a business' finances.
	Used to write reports in newpapers and on TV.

2

Sources of cash flow problems	To solve cash flow problems
Holding too much stock.	Offer discounts and promotions.
Allowing customers too much credit.	Reduce credit periods offered to customers.
Poor debt control.	Encourage debtors to pay promptly.
Borrowing at high interest rates.	Arrange a new source of finance.
Borrowing too much.	Sell unnecessary fixed assets.
Owner taking too many drawings.	Reduce owner's drawings.
Outright purchase of assets.	Purchase assets on hire purchase.

8   Human Resource Management

Intermediate 2

1a New ideas brought in.
Avoid friction between internal candidates.
Larger pool of potential candidates.

1b Newspaper adverts.
Specialist magazines.
Internet – own website or recruitment sites.
Job Centre.
Recruitment Agency.
Schools/Colleges/Universities.

2 Staff become more competent in their job.
Increased flexibility.
Increased staff motivation.
Increased productivity.
Change easier to introduce.
Improved image.
Less accidents.
Reduced waste.

3 Job title, working hours, wage/salary, holidays, pensions scheme, start date.

4

Equal Pay Act 1970	Employees should receive the same rate of pay where work of 'equal value' is undertaken.	
Sex Discrimination Act 1975	Prohibits discrimination in terms of recruitment on the grounds of:	sex or marital status.
Race Relations Act 1976		race, colour, nationality or ethnic origin.
Disability Discrimination Act 1995		someone being disabled.
Employment Equality (Religion or Belief) Regulations 2003		religion or belief.
Employment Equality (Age) Regulations 2006		age
Employment Rights Act 1996	States rights of employers and employees: Right to a Contract of Employment; Right to an itemised pay slip; Rights regarding Sunday working.	
National Minimum Wage Regulations 1999	States the minimum wage rates that must be paid to employees.	

Higher

1

Increase in part-time work	Staff work part of the working week. May be linked to the rise in women working. Can be permanent or temporary part-time. Office, shop and call centre workers often work part-time.
Increase in service sector	Increasing numbers of staff working in finance, retail and tourism. Matched by a decline in manufacturing industries. Rise in call centre working.
Increase in public sector	Increasing numbers of employees in teaching, NHS, police, local government, etc.

Increase in women working	Equality legislation.
	Increased access to flexible working.
	Increased access to childcare.
	Increase in service sector employment.
Increase in homeworking	Increased used of ICT.
	Staff want increased flexibility.

2 Identify a vacancy.
Conduct a job analysis.
Identify the duties, skills and responsibilities of the job.
Prepare a job description.
Prepare a person specification.
Advertise internally in staff newsletter, notice board, intranet or externally in newspaper, internet, job centre.
Go through application forms/CVs.
Attainment, aptitude, IQ, psychometric or medical tests or Assessment centre.
Interview.

3

Advantages	Disadvantages
Staff become better at their jobs.	Staff may leave after acquiring new skills.
Increased staff flexibility.	High cost of training.
Motivation increases.	Lost work time.
Staff become more productive.	Lost output.
Changes easier to introduce.	Staff may request pay rise.
Fewer accidents.	Quality of training must be high.
Reduced waste.	

4 Review of staff performance.
Normally carried out by line manager.
Focus on strengths and weaknesses.
Training needs may be highlighted.
Targets may be set.

Benefits:
Staff may get bonus.
May lead to promotion.
Improved morale.
Improved staff skills.

5 Negotiate with staff and trade unions over matters of joint interest.
Consult staff over major changes.
Worker directors – have a staff elected member sit on the Board of Directors to represent workers' opinions.
Works councils – have regular meetings with equal staff and manager representatives to discuss any changes taking place.
Quality circles - have staff meet regularly to discuss the work area they are involved in. Suggestions for improvement can be made and implemented.
Issue bonuses/financial incentives.
Provide a profit-sharing/share ownership scheme.
Conduct staff appraisals.
Organise team-building and social events.
Organise staff training.

Equal Pay Act 1970	Employees should receive the same rate of pay where work of 'equal value' is undertaken.	
Sex Discrimination Act 1975	Prohibits discrimination in terms of recruitment, promotion, conditions and dismissal on the grounds of:	sex or marital status.
Race Relations Act 1976		race, colour, nationality or ethnic origin.
Disability Discrimination Act 1995		someone being disabled.
Employment Equality (Religion or Belief) Regulations 2003		religion or belief.
Employment Equality (Age) Regulations 2006		age
Employment Rights Act 1996	States rights of employers and employees: Right to a Contract of Employment; Right to an itemised pay slip; Rights regarding Sunday working.	
National Minimum Wage Regulations 1999	States the minimum wage rates that must be paid to employees. There are 3 levels depending on the age of the employee.	
Offices, Shops and Railway Premises Act 1963	States the basic health and safety requirements that employers must meet regarding: temperatures, toilet facilities, space for staff.	
Health and Safety at Work Act 1974	States employer and employee responsibilities regarding health and safety. Employees to take care of their own and other's health and safety.	

ACKNOWLEDGEMENTS

Leckie & Leckie has made every effort to trace all copyright holders. If any have been inadvertently overlooked, we will be pleased to make the necessary arrangements. We would like to thank the following for their permission to reproduce material:

Empics for the 'Michelle Mone' image (page 17);

Chromepix/Alamy for the 'Domino's Pizza' image (page 18);

Corbis for the 'Video Conferencing' image (page 33);

Corbis for the 'Boardroom' image (page 39);

Corbis for the 'Decision Making' image (page 39);

Robert Harding for the 'Police' image (page 46);

Niall McDiarmid/Alamy for the 'M & S Shop Front' image (page 50);

Justin Kase/Alamy for the 'Market Researcher' image (page 56);

Corbis for the 'Shop Window Sale' (page 64);

The Scotsman Publications Ltd. for an extract adapted from a Scotland on Sunday article on 23/4/06 (www.scotlandonsunday.scotsman.com) (page 64);

Corbis for the 'Envelopes' image (page 67);

Empics for the 'Shopping Centre' image (page 68);

Corbis for the 'Production Line' image (page 84);

Stefan Sollfors/Alamy for the 'Joiner' image (page 84);

Corbis for the 'Job Interview' image (page 104);

Corbis for the 'Staff Training' image (page 104).

The following companies/individuals have very generously given permission to reproduce their copyright material free of charge:

Stagecoach Group for their logo (page 11);

CHAS for their logo and an extract adapted from www.chas.org.uk *and* www.oscr.org.uk (page 12);

MJM International for an extract adapted from www.ultimo.co.uk and www.michellemone.com (p17);

HMSO for e-commerce statistics adapted from Office of National Statistics © Crown Copyright. *Reproduced under the terms of the Click-Use Licence* (p 34);

Mackies for an image of their products and an extract from their website www.mackies.co.uk (page 58);

Irn Bru for an image of a can of Irn Bru (page 62);

Next for an image of their catalogue (page 67);

Dr. Matt Soar for an extract adapted *from* www.brandhype.org (p 71);

The Cake & Chocolate Shop for the 'Cake' image (page 82);

Dunlop Dairy for an image of their products (page 83);

Highland Spring for their logo and an extract (page 84);

Boyd Tunnock for the 'Tunnock's Teacake' image (page 85);

Unison for their logo (page 106);

NUS Scotland for their logo (page 106);

HMSO for the table 'Full Time & Part Time Earnings 2005' adapted from Annual Survey of Hours and Earnings 2005 by Office of National Statistics © Crown Copyright. *Reproduced under the terms of the Click-Use Licence* (p 110).